WRITING HORROR

WRITING HORROR

Edo van Belkom

Self-Counsel Press
(a division of)
International Self-Counsel Press
USA   Canada

Self-Counsel Press acknowledges the financial support of the Government of Canada
through the Book Publishing Industry Development Program for our publishing
activities.

Printed in Canada.

First edition: 2000

Canadian Cataloguing in Publication Data
van Belkom, Edo.
    Writing horror

    (Self-counsel writing series)
    ISBN 1-55180-281-3

    1. Horror tales — Authorship. I. Title. II. Series.
PN3377.5.H67V36 2000   808.3′8738   C00-910106-3

Self-Counsel Press
(a division of)
International Self-Counsel Press Ltd.

1704 N. State Street
Bellingham, WA 98225
USA

1481 Charlotte Road
North Vancouver, BC V7J 1H1
Canada

contents

Samples

Table

acknowledgments

I'd like to thank the following people: My editors at Self-Counsel Press: Judy Phillips who got the project started and Catherine Bennett who saw it through to the end; colleagues Crawford Kilian, Robin Bailey, Mort Castle, Amarantha Knight, Garrett Peck, Paula Guran, Robert J. Sawyer, Algis Budrys, and Brett Savory for bits of information and opinion along the way; and my beta tester, Michael Kelly, who helped make sure it all made sense.

I am grateful to all the interviewees: Douglas Clegg, Gary A. Braunbeck, Mike Ford, Stanley Wiater, Nancy Kilpatrick, Richard Laymon, Kathryn Ptacek, Don Hutchison, Ed Gorman, and S.P. Somtow, who gave up some of their precious time to enrich this book with their invaluable advice and experience.

And of course, thank you to my wife, Roberta, without whose help this — and all my other books — would never have been written.

A writer's life is short — limited to the life of the paper on which his words are inscribed, and the memory span of his readers. Paper is brittle and soon crumbles to dust, and the worms eat memories.

— ROBERT BLOCH

introduction

So, Who Wants to Be a Horror Writer?

Whenever I give a talk on the craft of writing (whether on horror, fantasy, short story, or just plain creative writing), I always begin with a question. And even though this is a book on the subject of writing, it has the feel — to me anyway — of a long talk. So I don't see any reason why I should begin the book any differently than I would a talk.

Who wants to be a horror writer?

Put up your hand.

Great.

Who wants to write horror fiction?

Go on, if that's you, then put up your hand.

"What?" you say, as you put up your hand again. "Isn't it the same thing?"

No, it is not.

It's one thing to want to be a writer. It looks like a great life: you work when you want to, you take it easy when you feel like it, you don't have to answer to anyone but yourself, and people will sometimes tell you how brilliant you are and how much they loved your stories. If you're lucky, sometimes they might even ask you for your autograph.

Yeah, being a writer's a real plum of a job, let me tell you.

But that's the only part that appeals to most people — seeing your name in print, having a book with your name on it on the shelf, winning an award, being featured in the newspaper.

Trouble is, none of that stuff comes until you've done the work.

The publication of my first short story collection, *Death Drives a Semi*, in October 1998, was a milestone in my writing career. Because I'd been inspired to try writing stories after reading (and loving) Ray Bradbury's collection *The October Country*, having my own collection published (20 stories, just like Bradbury) was the point at which I figured I'd reached some level of success. I had already published two novels, a book of nonfiction, and some 100 short stories, but a collection was what I'd always hoped for, and now here it was. I wanted to throw a big party to celebrate. With the help of my wonderfully supportive spouse (something a writer desperately needs), I launched the book in the theater of a local library branch. We invited hundreds of people (about 100 showed up), gave them wine and finger food, and I gave a reading of three stories from the book. We sold copies in the lobby, and I signed them all. It was an unforgettable night. A special night. Seeing me operate on that night, signing autographs, getting applause for my work, who wouldn't want to be a writer too?

Well, that night was the culmination of some eight years of hard work, rejection, emotional and financial struggle, and a lot of sweat and tears.

One night after eight years of work.

Not much of a payoff when you think of it.

So why do I do it? Why be a writer when I could do almost anything else and a) make more money, as well as b) suffer far less aggravation?

The answer is simple.

Because I have no choice in the matter.

I am driven to write. I must write.

Which brings me to my first point, which I will allow someone else to make for me. Gary Brandner said it best in his obscure novel, *Billy Lives!*, about a dead rock and roller. A character says, "Aspiring my ass.

You write or you don't. The curse of this profession is that it's so much more fun being a writer than it is writing."

I've never found a truer quote on the subject. Being a writer is fun. Writing is hard work.

I'm often contacted by people who see an article about me in the newspaper and call me up to say, "I'm writing a book and I want to know where to get it published."

I answer them by saying, "Finish writing it first."

They usually never do finish the book. After all, starting a book is easy. Finishing it is hard.

And getting it published is damn near impossible.

When I first began writing short stories, I was working as a reporter on a daily newspaper. I figured I'd try writing fiction for 10 or 20 years and if nothing happened in that time, then I'd spend my spare hours happily doing something — anything — else. It took about 4 years to sell my first story (which was reprinted in *Year's Best Horror Stories XX*, edited by Karl Edward Wagner) and a few more years of rejection to start selling on a somewhat regular basis. And even now, though people contact me for work (mostly short stories and articles), I still get rejected far more often than I like.

I often give a talk called "Thriving on Rejection." I explain that in my early years I would sell one story a year while having 54 others rejected — more than one a week. That sort of thing is pretty tough for anyone to take. I was also a member of a writers' group that met weekly to critique each other's manuscripts. That was tough too, because as much as I wanted to hear how wonderful my story was, nobody was going to give me that satisfaction, mainly because my story wasn't wonderful; it needed work, or it was just plain dumb. Those two years gave me a tough skin (another handy thing for a writer to develop) and helped me create a great metaphor for writers'-group critique sessions: workshop groups are like vampires, and having your manuscript work-shopped is like *opening a vein and handing out straws*.

If it sounds as if I'm trying to discourage you, perhaps I am. Whenever Harlan Ellison (a master of the science fiction, fantasy, and horror genres) teaches a class he tells his students flat out that if he can convince them that they're never going to make it as a writer, they were never meant to be writers in the first place.

In short, you've got to want it.

And want it bad.

Why? Because all along the way, editors and publishers are going to tell you "No," and they won't even tell you why. Taking rejection is a big part of becoming a writer. If you can't handle it, you'll never make it through the gauntlet that leads to publication.

But what if you don't have aspirations of becoming a professional writer? What if you just want to write stories for your own pleasure? If they get published, great; if not, oh well.

I say that's terrific. Having a full-time job and writing horror fiction on the side is probably the best way to go. That way, you'll be able to experience the ups and downs of the writing life without taking your quality of life — and that of your family — along for the ride. That's because horror is a tough market to crack these days. There are few high-paying markets for short fiction, and the novel market has dissolved into the mainstream. Horror novels still get published regularly, but the boom of the 1980s in which every publisher had to find three horror novels a month to publish, or else, is over.

So if you want to write horror, here are a few bits of advice:

- Read. Read a lot. Read inside the genre and out. Read fiction and nonfiction. Read the paper. Read anything and everything you can.

- Write. Write stories. Try writing a novel. Write poems. Write articles. Write some more stories. Write and write and write.

- Don't get discouraged. Remember that although John Saul's first published novel, *Suffer the Children*, was a bestseller, he wrote *ten* novels before a publisher said "Yes" to one of them.

- Read and write some more.

- Research the horror market, then send your stories and novels out to the editors and publishers you think might like what you're writing. You'll never know if you're any good or if you have any talent if you don't test your work in the marketplace. And you'll never sell anything that's sitting at the bottom of your desk drawer.

- Keep reading. Keep writing, and don't get discouraged.

If I've repeated myself here a few times, it's intentional. As you read through this book you'll find that I've repeated the point again, because it can't be stressed enough.

Writing is hard work, but perseverance is rewarded.

Now if I haven't totally discouraged you or scared you away, and you're still determined to come along for the ride, let's take a tour through the horror genre, find out how it works, and find out what's worked for me (and others). At some point, you might learn what will work for you.

And if I scare you any more along the way...

Great!

part one:

the horror genre

My theory is that if you're easily discouraged, you'd better not try to be a writer! You just keep on going, no matter how bad everyone says your work is, and no matter how many people say, "You really have to face up to reality: You just can't do this."

— JOHN SAUL

Basically, persist. And if anybody asked me, I would do my best to discourage them, because if I could discourage them, then they've got no business doing it because they're going against incredible odds.

— GAHAN WILSON

1
what is horror?

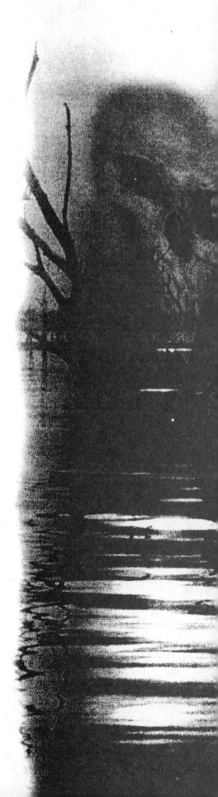

The Differences between Science Fiction, Fantasy, and Horror

Science fiction, fantasy, and horror are all very closely related. Each is part of the genre called speculative fiction, or SF for short. All three have speculation at their core, a single question: What if?

What if we were able to travel through space to other worlds?

What if dragons and unicorns were real, and wizards could cast spells?

What if the dead rose up from their graves with an insatiable hunger for human flesh?

Because they are so closely related, the lines between the genres are quite often blurred, and a work of horror ends up being disguised as science fiction. The first *Alien* film is a perfect example of this. The crew of a spaceship discover they have an unwanted guest on board — the alien of the title — and they must do their best to get rid of it before it gets rid of them. Replace the alien with any monster of your choice and the spaceship with a haunted castle, and you've got a classic tale of horror.

But despite the crossover between science fiction, fantasy, and horror, each one still contains key elements that set it apart from the others.

These have to do with the parts of the body and mind that each genre appeals to.

I don't think anyone would argue the statement that *science fiction is the genre of the mind*. It is an art form that makes you think, examining and solving problems by way of science and technology. In its classic form, science fiction requires that you take what is known in our world and extrapolate that knowledge to imagine what might happen in the future.

Carrying on with this notion, one could say that *fantasy is the genre of the heart*. Fantastic stories are the stuff that dreams are made of. Think of the Iowa farmer in W.P. Kinsella's *Shoeless Joe* (later made into the successful film *Field of Dreams*, starring Kevin Costner), who builds a baseball diamond in his cornfield and attracts the ghosts of long-dead ball players to play on it. Or consider the key ingredient in most heroic fantasy or tales of swords and sorcery — the never-ending battle between good and evil. Even this, in the *Star Wars* films, has been cloaked by the trappings of science fiction and the temptations of the dark side of the force.

So if science fiction is the genre of the mind, and fantasy is the genre of the heart, what might horror be?

One clue is what happens to you when you read a particularly chilling horror story. Your heart might begin to race, your breathing becomes more rapid, and tiny goose bumps rise up on your flesh, leaving you with a tingling feeling all over.

Horror is the genre of the senses.

The object of horror fiction is to elicit some sort of response from the reader. When it's good, horror can make your skin crawl, your pulse race, your body break out in a cold sweat, and your hair stand on end. And even when it's bad, horror can elicit a response. Oftentimes horror writers resort to the gross-out — truly ghastly images and occurrences explained in excruciatingly vivid detail. While not as elegant as shadows across the moors or the whisper of death through the trees, the gross-out is still an integral part of horror because of the response it elicits: it turns your stomach.

Horror Movies versus Horror Fiction

People usually judge the merits of a particular genre by its lowest common denominator. For example, those without a genuine interest in science fiction might refer to the genre as sci-fi (the term used to describe it in the pulp era) and treat it with disdain because their only exposure to it has been through what they've seen on late-night television. But while B-movies about bug-eyed monsters and Mars needing women are part of the science fiction genre, they are not its shining example.

The same is true in the horror genre. The most easily identifiable icons in horror these days are the monsters that were popular in 1980s movies like *Friday the 13th* and *Nightmare on Elm Street.* While Jason and Freddy are credible movie monsters providing shock entertainment through more than a dozen movies (and the string of lesser imitations that tried to cash in on their popularity), they aren't the best the horror genre has to offer. So when people say, "I don't like horror," they're often saying it with these film characters in mind.

Would they say the same thing about the movie *Jaws*? You might not think of it as a horror film, but how else would you describe a tale about a monstrous shark terrorizing a peaceful resort community off the New England coast? It's a monster movie, plain and simple.

All of which brings us to horror fiction — novels and short stories — which can be every bit as diverse as horror in film. Many readers say they don't like the horror genre because they don't like reading about supernatural monsters or psychopaths killing people in gory baths of blood and guts. Such splatter *is* part of the horror genre, but it's not all there is to it. Horror is also Robert Bloch's *Psycho,* Thomas Harris's, *The Silence of the Lambs,* Bram Stoker's *Dracula,* and Mary Shelley's *Frankenstein.* These are classics, and might even be favorites of someone who emphatically states they do not like horror.

The next time someone says to you, "I don't like horror," ask him or her what type of horror he or she means. If the only response is that he or she doesn't like Jason and Freddy, consider it an opportunity to educate and inform a latent fan of the genre.

Getting a Solid Grounding in the Genre

Obviously there is a lot more to horror than what can be seen on the silver screen. Likewise, there is a lot more to horror fiction than Stephen King, Dean Koontz, Anne Rice, and Clive Barker. While these authors are the genre's bestsellers — not to mention bestselling authors in *any* genre — and their contribution to horror is an important one, they are only a small part of the genre's overall scope.

Most people's first exposure to horror stories was probably in the form of fairy tales and nursery rhymes.

Fairy tales as horror stories?

What else might you call a story in which a girl named Little Red Riding Hood is eaten by a wolf and has to be cut out of its stomach by a woodsman?

Or what about a story of two children named Hansel and Gretel who get lost in the forest, are befriended by a witch who wishes to eat them in a pie, and whose only escape is to push her into the fire?

Nancy Baker, author of such vampire novels as *The Night Inside* and *A Terrible Beauty,* claims that the first horror story she can recall is "The Tale of Squirrel Nutkin" by Beatrix Potter, a story in which Squirrel Nutkin avoids being skinned alive by an owl named Old Brown by pulling off his own tail.

The truth is, most people have been exposed to and have enjoyed tales of horror throughout their lives but haven't recognized them as horror per se. Indeed, the horror genre didn't even exist as a publishing category until the late 1970s and early 1980s, when every major publishing house started up a horror line in an attempt to duplicate the success of Stephen King's early novels.

But given that a lot of horror doesn't come in a package that's wrapped in a bloody bow with the word HORROR stamped on its sides, how do you go about getting a solid grounding in the horror genre?

Simple. You read and read and read a whole lot of horror stories and novels.

If you want to write horror, you have to read it. Not just King and Koontz, but the writers who influenced them as well. That means going to your local library or bookstore and scouring the racks for story collections and novels by the likes of Bram Stoker, Edgar Allan Poe, H.P. Lovecraft, Robert Bloch, Ray Bradbury, and Richard Matheson. When you're well versed in their work, move up to more contemporary authors like Jack Ketchum, Richard Laymon, Gary Brandner, Ray Garton, Bentley Little, Joe R. Lansdale, Norman Partridge, Matthew J. Costello, and Ed Gorman.

Sounds like a lot of work, doesn't it? But writing horror fiction well requires that you do a bit of work, just like any other profession. You wouldn't start practicing law without reading a few books first, and you certainly wouldn't practice dentistry without a certain amount of study and training.

Fortunately, you don't have to read everything by everyone to get a sense of what the horror genre is about. You can read a selection from each writer, discover the authors you like best, then read everything by that author. Eventually you'll discover the things that make them good at what they do. You might also learn to recognize what doesn't work and decide what kind of writing style best suits your own talents.

You can also cut down on the reading you'll have to do by finding a few of the "best books" lists compiled by respected authors and critics in the horror field. One of the best such guides is *Horror: The 100 Best Books*, edited by Stephen Jones and Kim Newman, which features mini-essays on each of the top 100 horror books by some of the top writers, editors, and critics in the genre today. The list begins with Christopher Marlowe's *The Tragical History of Doctor Faustus*, published in 1592, and ends with Ramsey Campbell's 1987 story collection *Dark Feasts*. In between are such works as Shakespeare's *The Tragedy of Macbeth*, Henry James's *The Turn of the Screw*, and *Lord of the Flies* by William Golding. If the top 100 aren't enough, the book also includes a comprehensive recommended reading list with works dating back as far as 458 B.C.

Two other books that feature similar lists of best books are *Faces of Fear* by Douglas E. Winter and *Danse Macabre* by Stephen King. Obviously, you won't be able to read all the books on the lists, so if you have only a limited amount of time to invest, try reading a few of the books that appear on more than one of the lists.

Avoiding What's Been Done to Death

Aspiring writers often think their ideas are absolutely original; so original, in fact, that they don't want to tell anyone about them for fear that some unscrupulous writer might steal their ideas. Such things have happened in literary circles over the years, but far less often than people think. The truth is, it happens so seldomly that it's not worth worrying about.

What's more common is that an aspiring writer's new ideas turn out actually to be quite old and tired. For example, almost every writer has at one point or another thought about writing a story about a vampire with AIDS. If you aren't very well read in the genre you might think this is quite an original idea. After all, AIDS is in the news and vampires are popular. All of that is true, but such stories were written before most people knew about AIDS, and since then every variation on the theme has been explored in great detail. What's needed in such instances is for the writer to go past that first (easy) idea and to come up with a new twist on an old idea. I confess to have written one vampire-AIDS story, "Letting Go," about a compassionate vampire who sucks the life — rather than the blood — out of AIDS victims to put an end to their suffering. Sure, it's vampires and AIDS, but, given the subject matter, not a story one might expect.

A Few Words With...

Nancy Kilpatrick

on vampires

EDO VAN BELKOM: There seems to be no end to the popularity of vampires. How do you explain their seeming immortality?

NANCY KILPATRICK: The vampire is an archetype that permeates every culture, from the beginning of recorded history — *The Epic of Gilgamesh* talks of a vampire in the form of a "death-bringer." Because we are dealing with an archetype — meaning, the energy represents a basic pattern in the universe — the vampire can never go out of style. Every culture sees this predatory energy in its own way, so the vampire might consume anything: blood, energy, dreams, fears, talent, you name it. And the vampire itself can be anything from a physical being to a spirit form, it can be human, animal, plant, inanimate object, other... One thing about an archetypal energy is that it is not the form that matters but what is important is capturing the essence of the energy by being true to the archetype and what it means, which involves the reason why it effects human beings so strongly.

EDO VAN BELKOM: Do you find that new writers often think they've reinvented the wheel, when all they've really done is come up with an idea that's already been done to death?

NANCY KILPATRICK: Absolutely. And the reason is that they don't read. If writers read in an area where they want to write, they quickly discover what has been done before. A writer's job is to add to the body of work that exists, not rehash it. Now, of course all readers have not read everything, and are not up on the latest trends, but you can bet that good editors at publishing houses know what's been done before and what hasn't, and they are not buying last year's ideas. One thing you notice in small press publications is the same ideas over and over. I'm not speaking of all small presses, but it is common enough that you can start a story and think, so-and-so wrote this five years ago! Major houses are quite different. They are looking for the unusual, for the most part. Unusual, but still plausible.

EDO VAN BELKOM: Is there any territory that's still unexplored in terms of vampires, or are we closing in on the saturation point?

NANCY KILPATRICK: I'd say there is still unexplored territory but not much, at least not as we in the west conceive of the vampire. There have been innovations, some space vampires and some psychic vampires that have pushed the envelope. And a few stories have seeped into English literature from other cultures, creating a fresh approach. But until western culture moves along and we get a grip on a different vampiric image, we are stuck with the Victorian image which came out of Polidori's *The Vampire* and Prest's *Varney the Vampire* and then moved to the feminine version in LeFanu's *Carmilla* and finally culminated in Stoker's *Dracula* in 1897. This is the aristocratic vampire. And although there have been novels, for example, *Salem's Lot*, and many stories and movies which show the vampire as a hideous, corrupted corpse back from the dead and not very appealing, the trend has been towards the sophisticated, cultured vampire, which formerly was romantic and has in the last couple of decades become erotic in nature. And that has been done to death, if you'll excuse the pun. What we need are a few writers to take the vampire into the next millennium.

Nancy Kilpatrick is the author of the Power of the Blood series (Child of the Night; Near Death; Reborn), *the novelization of the vampire musical* Dracul, *and the* Vampire: The Masquerade *gaming novel* As One Dead. *In addition, she has authored two collections of vampire stories,* Sex & the Single Vampire *and* Endorphins, *written two erotic vampire novels, and edited the erotic vampire anthology* Love Bites. *She teaches a course in Writing Vampire Fiction on the Internet and can be contacted via her Web site:* <www.sff.net/people/nancyk>.

2
HORROR SUBGENRES

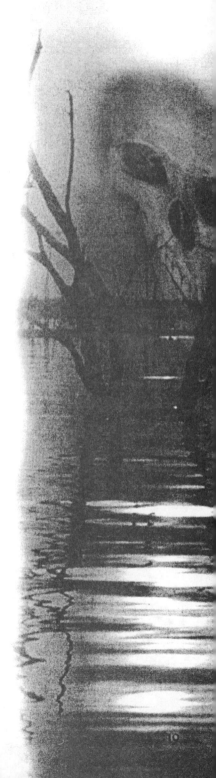

Horror is an emotional state: it is the hair rising up on the back of your neck, your heart leaping up into your throat, your stomach turning at the sight of something utterly disgusting. That's one of the reasons it can so easily be crossed with many other genres. An emotional element can always be inserted into another genre.

But horror is also a genre of literature. It wasn't always a genre unto itself, but became so in the late 1970s and early 1980s with the success of such authors as Stephen King, Peter Straub, and Anne Rice.

Before that time, works of horror were published as part of the mainstream or perhaps as works of fantasy. There was no horror genre in 1818 when Mary Shelley published Frankenstein, and almost 80 years later, when Bram Stoker published Dracula in 1897, there was still no such thing as a horror genre. But in the middle of the 20th century horror fiction publishing blossomed, with magazines like Weird Tales enjoying a long, successful run, publishing the works of such writers as Robert E. Howard, A. Merritt, August Derleth, and, of course, H.P. Lovecraft. Later it embraced the writings of Ray Bradbury, Robert Bloch, Richard Matheson, and Fritz Leiber, even though some of these people were primarily known as science fiction writers.

Indeed, at the 1998 Bram Stoker Award banquet in New York City, when science fiction writer Jack Williamson stepped up to the podium to accept his lifetime achievement award from the Horror Writers Association, he said, "I didn't know I was a horror writer." The reason it came as a surprise to Williamson was because horror creeps silently across the genres like a shadow creature with far-reaching tendrils. It takes what it wants, brings it back to its lair, and nestles it in among the many other things that make up its large and diverse cache of literary works.

So whenever people say to you, "I don't like horror," ask which kind of horror they mean.

If they ask you what you're talking about, consider it an invitation to educate them.

Classic Monsters

This subgenre includes all the monsters you readily associate with the horror genre, such as vampires, werewolves, the Frankenstein monster, ghosts, ghouls, and zombies, as well as a few that are on the fringe, like *The Creature from the Black Lagoon*. Although there was a film made of *The Mummy* in 1999, that classic monster seems, for the most part, to have fallen from grace, while others like vampires and werewolves have found new life as we enter a new millennium.

The vampire appears to be the monster with the most legs and is really a subgenre unto itself (see section below). And like the vampire mythos is the werewolf mythos, which has also been able to change with the times, but to a lesser extent. Lycanthropes were devised back when people lived a lot closer to the soil. They changed from people into forms that represented the destructive forces of those times. In Europe and England they turned into wolves and vampire bats, while in Scandinavia it was werebears. In Malaya and India it was weretigers and weresnakes, but in Africa it was werehyenas, werebuffaloes, and wereleopards. In each case it was the creature that took the greatest toll on the common people's lives and property. A classic update of this concept can be found in Joe R. Lansdale's *Batman* novel *Captured by the Engines*, in which a man is cursed with the ability to change into a fearsome, raging automobile — a werecar.

Selected authors and works featuring classic monsters

Gary Brandner, *The Howling* series

Tanya Huff, *Blood Lines*

Stephen King, *Cycle of the Werewolf*

Fritz Leiber, *Conjure Wife*

Clare McNally, *Ghost House*

Byron Preiss, ed., *The Ultimate Werewolf*

Mary Shelley, *Frankenstein*

Edo van Belkom, *Wyrm Wolf*

Jack Williamson, *Darker Than You Think*

Vampires

The vampire myth has proven to be the one most readily adaptable to the changing social climate of our times. What began as a hideous parasitic creature in the lore of many cultures around the world turned into the noble and romantic figure of Stoker's Dracula. Today, gone for the most part is the monster's religious connection; very few vampires in modern fiction can be scared off with holy water and a cross. Writers have been able to come up with some terrific new twists though, such as in David Dvorkin's *Insatiable*, in which a bunch of vampire groupies live to have the blood sucked from their bodies as a sort of ultimate thrill.

Selected authors and works featuring vampires

Stephen King, *Salem's Lot*

Richard Laymon, *Bite*

Kyle Marffin, *Carmilla: The Return*

Richard Matheson, *I Am Legend*

Anne Rice, *Interview with the Vampire*

Jeff Rice, *The Night Stalker*

Bram Stoker, *Dracula*

F. Paul Wilson, *The Keep*

I use the vampires as metaphorical figures to talk about life itself: what we don't know about it and what we must believe about it.

— ANNE RICE

A Few Words With...

Stanley Wiater

On Writing Horror Nonfiction

EDO VAN BELKOM: You are one of the most prominent writers of horror nonfiction working in the field today. How did you get started, and how did it grow into your full-time job?

STANLEY WIATER: I've been a journalist all my life, selling my first magazine articles while still in high school. I worked as an arts and entertainment reporter for a decade after college, then began contributing to horror magazines both in the States and abroad. I began my book career by compiling collections of the very same interviews I had sold to various newspapers and magazines. Horror journalism became my niche once I realized no one else was even attempting to work in it full time. Thanks to the Internet, I now sell worldwide.

EDO VAN BELKOM: What different types of nonfiction work do you do and which do you enjoy the most?

STANLEY WIATER: Primarily Q & A interviews or profiles. I also do the occasional article, essay, and book review. My two works in progress, *The Films of Wes Craven* and *The Stephen King Universe,* are both major critical studies. But I still enjoy the one-on-one interviews the most — it's a joy getting paid to tell someone you greatly admire to spill their guts for you!

EDO VAN BELKOM: Would you recommend to a new writer writing nonfiction as a good way to advance a fiction writing career?

STANLEY WIATER: Absolutely. It's a wonderful way to learn the business of writing and how to separate your personal feelings about your work from the often impersonal world of publishing. It took me ten years to sell my first short story, but in that time I had sold enough nonfiction to fill a couple of volumes. The point is, I learned so much about publishing in the interim that I could be self-employed as a journalist by day and still write my fiction by night.

———————

Stanley Wiater is the author or editor of eight books, including the Bram Stoker Award winning books Dark Dreamers: Conversations with the Masters of Horror *and* Dark Thoughts: On Writing, Advice and Commentary from Fifty Masters of Fear and Suspense *in which many of the quotes in this book first appeared. He recently collaborated with photographer Beth Gwinn for a celebration of the 100 greatest talents in horror,* Dark Dreamers: Facing the Masters of Fear. *His Web site address is: <www.alteredearth.com/wiater/wiater.htm>.*

Cthulhu Mythos

The Cthulhu mythos is the creation of H.P. Lovecraft, a brilliant horror writer who penned countless stories for *Weird Tales* in his brief, but remarkable lifetime. The Cthulhu stories began in 1928 with the publication of "The Call of Cthulhu" in *Weird Tales*. Lovecraft outlined the legend in the story, and explained it here in a letter to a friend:

> *All my stories, unconnected as they may be, are based on the fundamental lore or legend that this world was inhabited at one time by another race who, in practicing Black Magic, lost their foothold and were expelled, yet live on outside, ever ready to take possession of this Earth again.*

Cthulhu mythos stories are somewhat old-fashioned by today's standards, but nevertheless enjoy some popularity with die-hard Cthulhu fans. There is even a publisher, Chaosium Inc., that publishes an entire line of Cthulhu Mythos books, ranging from older works in the mythos by writers like Lovecraft and Robert Bloch to new works by younger authors in honor of Lovecraft's legacy.

Selected authors and works in the Cthulhu mythos

Scott D. Anoilowski, ed., *Cthulhu's Heirs*

Robert Bloch, *Mysteries of the Worm*

H.P. Lovecraft, *The Lurking Fear, The Outsider, Cry Horror!* (But almost any Lovecraft will do.)

Brian Lumley, *The Compleat Crow, Hero of Dreams*

Robert M. Price, ed., *The Hastur Cycle, Shrub-Niggurath Cycle*

Quiet Horror

Quiet horror relies on mood and atmosphere more than anything else for its chills. It is, above all else, low-key, suggestive, and understated. Instead of the monster jumping out of the closet, there is a shadow creeping across the wall. Instead of the rabid dog gnawing on your leg, there are the fingers of a cold, cold hand slowly closing around your neck. And instead of an explosion at the climax, there is a cool breeze that snuffs out a candle. This subgenre could almost be called "classic horror" since it relies on — and expands upon — all of the classic images of the horror genre.

This sort of horror also requires a deft hand and considerable writing talent, since stories and novels of quiet horror are about slow tours through the graveyard rather than about flesh-eating corpses rising up from their graves. They have to be extremely well written to be effective and maintain a reader's interest.

Selected authors and works of quiet horror

Dennis Etchison, *The Dark Country*

John Farris, *When Michael Calls*

Charles L. Grant, *The Pet, The Hour of the Oxrun Dead*

Shirley Jackson, *The Haunting of Hill House*

Peter Straub, *Ghost Story*

T.M. Wright, *Strange Seed, A Manhattan Ghost Story*

Splatterpunk

Splatterpunk is everything that quiet horror is not. In fact, it's the exact opposite. It is bloody, gory, in-your-face, and violent, the more blood and guts the better. This school of horror writing graduated onto the scene on the heels of such films as *The Texas Chainsaw Massacre*, and the *Friday the 13th* and *Nightmare on Elm Street* series of films. The thrust of this type of fiction was to be as graphic and gory as possible. The "splatterpunk" name was a parallel to the "cyberpunk" movement happening at the same time in science fiction. Both movements seem to have come and gone, and while some authors still publish overly violent horror, the splatterpunk label has passed out of favor with the majority of horror writers and readers. As B-movie film reviewer Joe Bob Briggs often stated in his reviews, "I am violently opposed to the use of chainsaws, power drills, tire tools, rubber hoses, brass knuckles, barbed wire, hypodermics, embalming needles, or poleaxes against women, unless it is necessary to the plot."

Selected authors and works of splatterpunk

Jack Ketchum, *Off Season*

Ed Lee, *Ghouls, The Bighead*

Paul M. Sammon, ed., *Splatterpunks: Extreme Horror*

David J. Schow, *The Kill Riff*

John Skipp and Craig Spector, *The Light at the End, The Clean-up*; eds., *Book of the Dead* and *Still Dead: Book of the Dead 2*

Psychological Horror

Psychological horror is all about madness and mad people, and is usually set in the modern day.

Psychologically unbalanced people are a staple of the horror genre, and there are many excellent examples of them in the works of two writers with similar-sounding names: Robert Bloch and Lawrence Block.

Robert Bloch, of course, wrote the novel *Psycho*, which Alfred Hitchcock turned into a famous suspense film. However, Bloch wrote plenty of other great psychological horror stories, most notably about one of the original psychos, Jack the Ripper.

Lawrence Block, known mostly as a mystery writer, is another gifted author of psychological horror. His story "The Tulsa Experience" is, I think, one of the best psycho stories of all time, and his novel *Hitman* is at once a complex journey into the mind of a killer and a sympathetic tale of someone who's just trying to make a living doing the only thing he happens to be good at.

If you're still unclear about what psychological horror is, think Ed Gein, David Berkowitz, and the Unabomber and you'll start to get the idea.

Selected authors and works of psychological horror

Robert Bloch, *Psycho, Psycho II,* "Yours Truly, Jack the Ripper"

Lawrence Block, *Hitman, Some Days You Get the Bear*

Martin H. Greenberg, ed., *Robert Bloch's Psychos*

Thomas Harris, *The Silence of the Lambs, Hannibal*

L. Ron Hubbard, *Fear*

Rex Miller, *Slob*

Occult/Supernatural Horror

As the word occult suggests, this type of horror delves into black magic, ancient religions, and deals with the devil. During horror's boom period in the 1980s, several publishers flirted with the idea of producing lines of strictly occult horror in addition to their regular horror titles, but this notion never really took hold.

Supernatural horror is any type of horror that occurs outside of our known universe, where the rules of the normal world need not apply. It includes any sort of ghosts, demons, or otherworldly monsters, especially those called into existence by the actions of one on the real-world side of the fence. These actions usually take the form of an elaborate ritual (or an accidental one) that results in the unleashing of some otherworldly power such as a poltergeist.

Although not exactly horror or prose fiction, a terrific example of what is meant by the occult can be seen in the three Indiana Jones films, especially the second installment, *Indiana Jones and the Temple of Doom.*

Selected authors and works of occult/supernatural horror

William Peter Blatty, *The Exorcist*

Gary Brandner, *Hellborn*

James Herbert, *The Spear*

Andrew Neiderman, *Love Child, After Life*

Oscar Wilde, *The Picture of Dorian Grey*

J.N. Williamson, *The Monastery*

Dark Fantasy

Dark fantasy is often a term used to describe all types of horror. It is used mostly by those who don't want to use the dreaded "H" word. Of course, most horror — with the exception of the psychological brand — has some element of fantasy to it. However, dark fantasy can best be described as any horror story or horrific tale containing elements of traditional fantasy but that does not include vampires, werewolves, or ghosts.

Think of Robert E. Howard's immortal creation, *Conan, the Barbarian*, and you have a very good idea of what dark fantasy is all about. Conan is a sword-wielding adventurer who is confronted by mystical, magical monsters at every turn, none of which are the sort of classic icons of the horror genre mentioned earlier. Instead they are monsters that have elements of the Earth, Wind, and Fire in them, or dragons, animated skeletons, evil genies, and trolls.

A more modern version of dark fantasy is the Dark Knight himself, Batman. In this case, the dark part is more important than the fantasy part, but many supernatural events still occur in Gotham City, making this a good example of the subgenre.

Selected authors and works of dark fantasy

Robert E. Howard, *Conan, the Barbarian* (Other Conan stories are collected under various titles, with several different co-authors.)

Joe R. Lansdale, *Batman: Captured by the Engines*

Darrell Schweitzer, *The Mask of the Sorcerer*

Erotic Horror

Erotic horror has become one of the most popular subgenres of horror in the past few years, with dozens of anthologies and novels filling up the shelves. One of the reasons for the success of erotic horror is that horror easily lends itself to tales of sex and lust. Both horror and erotica provide the reader with an emotional charge. With horror, you're scared, while with erotica you're turned on; and when erotic horror works best, you're both afraid and just a little bit turned on. A lot of vampire fiction falls into the realm of erotic horror since the vampire is usually a romantic figure.

There are basically two kinds of erotic horror. The first kind is horror stories that have some sexual content or subject matter such as you might find in the *Hot Blood* anthology series. The stories don't necessarily have to be sexy or even provide a turn-on to the reader, but they must deal in some way with sex and adult situations. (For this reason, it's often called "sexual horror" rather than "erotic horror.") The second kind is erotic stories that are just a little bit dangerous, more graphic and explicit and bordering on what some might call pornography.

Selected authors and works of erotic horror

Ramsey Campbell, *Scared Stiff*

Jeff Gelb, Michael Garrett, eds., *The Hot Blood Series, Vols. 1—10*

Amarantha Knight, ed., *Flesh Fantastic, Seductive Spectres,*

Demon Sex, Love Bites

Michelle Slung, ed., *I Shudder at Your Touch*

Lucy Taylor, *Unnatural Acts and Other Stories*

Thomas Tessier, *Finishing Touches*

A Few Words With...

Nancy Kilpatrick

ON WRITING EROTIC HORROR

EDO VAN BELKOM: Why do you think erotica has had such a successful union with the horror genre?

NANCY KILPATRICK: It's a natural marriage. The history of human sexuality is impregnated with guilt that often leads to death, or worse — we have always taken a grim approach to a natural function. The best horror tends to be both visceral and psychological; sensuality blends nicely with both realms. And we humans seem to prefer our sex a tad scary, and for our fears to have impact, we need them to tap both the psychological and the physical so that they are tied up with our drive toward pleasure. Shrewd writers capitalize on this. For one thing, it's fun and challenging to blend genres. Also, in today's market, it makes good marketing sense.

EDO VAN BELKOM: Have you found anything to be off limits or taboo in terms of subject matter?

NANCY KILPATRICK: Not really. As a writer, I've had only one story pulled — by the publishing house, not by the editor. As an editor, none of my publishers have rejected any material I've selected. There are tricky subjects, of course, but good writing can deal with even the most taboo material, like incest, snuff, and bestiality. At the turn of the millennium, we have collectively experienced it all, at least vicariously, and people are jaded. One of the challenges for a writer is to come up with a view of material that actually "melts the frozen sea within," as Kafka put it. A story evocative and vivid, one that cuts deep enough that the reader will again feel something. In the case of erotic horror, the writer aims for feelings of arousal and revulsion combined. No easy task. But pulled off successfully, it becomes a remarkable and rewarding story for both the writer and the reader.

EDO VAN BELKOM: As the editor of several anthologies, is there any aspect of erotic horror in which you think writers most often miss the mark?

NANCY KILPATRICK: The biggest problem with blending any genres is to make the story work in both worlds. This is simply good writing. The story itself becomes a double entendre. It can be read as horror or erotica, and it works for either or both. Writers usually slight one genre in favor of the other, so the story reads as either erotic or horrific but not erotic horror, which is a hybrid unto itself.

For more information on Nancy Kilpatrick, see pages 17–18.

Dark Suspense

Like dark fantasy, dark suspense is often used as an alternative to the word horror as the name of the genre. But unlike dark fantasy, dark suspense is a much more limiting term and deals with a much smaller body of work.

Suspense refers to works that have no supernatural element, no truly horrific element (such as an evil monster or blow-by-blow accounts of murders), but in which great harm can happen to the characters at any moment. Quite often, the threat comes from a psychopath or stalker who is outside (but always looking in on) the realm of the main characters of the story or book. The suspense develops as we follow the lives of characters we care about as they unknowingly come within a hair's breadth of their deaths. These books are also a mainstay of the mystery genre, especially when instead of a family in peril, the reader is engaged in the plight of the investigator entrusted with the job of stopping the killer before more innocent people are murdered.

Selected authors and works of suspense

Robert Bloch, *Night World*

Matthew J. Costello, *Homecoming, See How She Runs*

Ed Gorman, *Black River Falls, Cage of Night*

Jack Ketchum, *Joyride, Stranglehold*

Joe R. Lansdale, *Act of Love*

Richard Laymon, *Midnight's Lair, Tread Softly*

Michael Slade, *Ghoul, Headhunter*

Young Adult/Juvenile Horror

Young adult horror is exactly what it says it is: horror for young adults.

While adult horror as a publishing genre has been in decline, young adult horror has enjoyed enormous popularity through many different series and authors. For a time, R.L. Stine was the best-selling author in the world with sales of his *Goosebumps* (juvenile) and *Fear Street* (young adult) series counted in increments of millions. Christopher Pike is another author who has enjoyed widespread success.

Publishers had hoped that the great numbers of young adult horror readers would continue their horror reading into adulthood, but so far that hasn't been the case. R.L. Stine even produced an adult horror novel, but its reception was lukewarm. The general consensus is that the wave of popularity enjoyed by this subgenre has crested, making way, perhaps, for science fiction and the currently popular *Animorphs*, by K.A. Applegate.

Selected authors and works of young adult/juvenile horror

Bruce Coville, *Bruce Coville's Book of...* (Series of anthologies)

Lois Duncan, *I Know What You Did Last Summer*

Christopher Pike, *The Last Vampire, Remember Me*

R.L. Stine, *Goosebumps, Fear Street*

Edo van Belkom, ed., *Be Afraid!* (My own YA horror anthology, Tundra Books, Oct 2000)

The above is only a brief synopsis of some of the subgenres of horror. It's worth mentioning that some authors, such as Jack Ketchum and Richard Laymon, are listed in more than one subgenre as their work — and the work of many horror authors — covers a lot of territory. Very few authors produce just a single type of horror.

If you want to write horror, try reading in the different subgenres to find the one you like best. After getting a good feel for that subgenre, you'll be ready to write about something with which you're familiar.

3
story format

If you're thinking of writing tales of horror, your first inclination might be to write the kind of horror you most enjoy yourself. You might want to write a screenplay because you love watching horror movies, or you might want to write a novel because you enjoy reading books by Stephen King and Dean Koontz, or you might want to write some short stories because you've always admired the tales of terror by Ray Bradbury, Robert Bloch, or Roald Dahl.

The choice is yours to make, and your preference will likely be determined by the format you read most. However, if you don't have your heart set on one particular format, there are a few things you should consider before beginning.

Horror Short Stories versus Horror Novels

A horror novel runs about 60,000 words and up, which means when it's published it fills 200 or more pages in a printed book. It takes a long time to write that much, a commitment of at least a few months and quite possibly a couple of years. Even when you're finished, the chances of selling your very first novel are pretty slim. (Most authors never sell their first novel. Their first *published* novel is usually their third or fourth attempt at writing one.)

The conventional wisdom for aspiring writers is for you to learn your craft writing short stories before trying to write full-length novels. There are several reasons for this:

- A novel is at least 60,000 words long, while an average horror story is between 3,000 and 5,000 words. In the time it takes to write one horror novel, you can write 15 to 20 horror stories and get the benefit of having done something 15 to 20 times, as opposed to having done something once.

- You are more likely to sell a short story than a novel. There are dozens of markets for horror stories out there publishing hundreds of stories each year. In the early years, the encouragement of having sold a short story and seeing it in print will keep you writing, while a form rejection on a novel you spent a year on might just make you cry "Uncle!" and shut down your word processor.

- The craft of short story writing is much more demanding than that of novel writing. In short stories every word counts for something, while in a novel you have more room to indulge yourself. Once you've mastered short story writing, chances are you'll then be better able to tackle your first novel.

- With several short fiction sales to your credit, you'll have a better chance of attracting the interest of an editor at a publishing house when you send a query letter, or of the agent you approach to represent your novel. Some publication credits in the short fiction field might ultimately help you sell a novel sooner than you would otherwise, because few editors will buy a first novel from someone with absolutely *no* publication credits.

To help explain these points, I offer this excerpt from Joe R. Lansdale's second short story collection, *Bestsellers Guaranteed*, published in 1993 by Ace, which is a revised edition of the 1991 Pulphouse collection, *Stories by Mama Lansdale's Youngest Boy.*

> *Early in my career, as with most writers, I found it very difficult to get my work published, and because of this it was less daunting to spend a few days to a week on a short story instead of months on a novel that might be rejected. A short investment of time and the fact that I could have a dozen or more short stories working for me instead of one novel was very appealing. There was also the fact that I needed money, and though I wasn't*

making a killing with the sales of my short stories, fifty dollars here, a hundred dollars there was preferable to all the rejects I got on novels like Act of Love, Dead in the West, *and* The Nightrunners.

The novels Lansdale mentions above eventually sold and have been tremendously successful. His career is now flourishing, and in addition to such recent novels as *Rumble Tumble* and *Bad Chili* he has written comic scripts, screenplays, plays, and nonfiction. But no matter how successful other aspects of Lansdale's career are, it all began with the writing of some excellent short fiction.

Of course, this is only one way to do it. Granted, it is the way *many* writers start out, but it's not the way *all* writers do — John Saul being just one example of a writer who took a different path. If you have your heart set on writing novels and can't see yourself doing anything different, then start working on that novel. But if you're unsure about where to begin, try writing short pieces and work your way toward the novel.

What Works Best for a Tale of Horror?

Short story or novel? that is the question.

Does your idea have enough legs for a novel? Might it not be better suited to a short story, novelette, or novella? Though it might make for a topic of some spirited discussion among horror writers, it's my opinion that tales of horror work best at shorter lengths. That's not to say it's impossible to write an excellent horror novel — many authors have done it with regularity — but you have an infinitely better chance of writing a really good horror short story than of writing a really good horror novel.

While it isn't hard to list some truly excellent horror novels — *Ghost Story* by Peter Straub, *The Exorcist* by William Peter Blatty, *The Haunting of Hill House* by Shirley Jackson — it is just as easy to come up with an extensive list of excellent shorter works of horror such as "The Picture of Dorian Grey" by Oscar Wilde, "The Pit and The Pendulum" and "The Raven" by Edgar Allan Poe, "The Turn of the Screw" by Henry James, "The Strange Case of Dr. Jekyll and Mr. Hyde" by Robert Louis Stephenson... The list could go on and on. The abundance of classic short stories is something quite unique to the horror genre, and with good reason.

Novels are work and plenty of it... A short story, on the other hand, can be held complete in the mind and written in a single session. I wouldn't suggest for a moment that it's easier to write salable short stories than novels — it's probably the other way around — but it's a good deal less exhausting and it's often more fun.

— LAWRENCE BLOCK

A Few Words With...

Richard Laymon

on horror novels versus short stories

EDO VAN BELKOM: After writing 30 novels and more than 65 short stories, do you approach the writing of a story any differently than the writing of a novel?

RICHARD LAYMON: Whether hoping to write a short story or a novel, I start out the same way, by trying to come up with a strange, appealing situation. I search my mind for a good "What if?" Once the "What if?" is discovered, I try to focus the plot on a very precise point in time when writing a short story. If I want to turn the "What if" into a novel, I work on expanding the idea and trying to figure out all the various places I might go with it.

EDO VAN BELKOM: Which do you enjoy more, writing short stories or writing novels?

RICHARD LAYMON: I suppose I enjoy writing novels more than short stories. Short stories are easy and quick to write, usually taking me only two or three days to finish a first draft. I like the way that short stories are neat and concise. When writing a novel, I usually spend the better part of a year. So writing a novel is vastly more difficult than writing a short story. Novels, however, are also more rewarding. With a novel, there is plenty of room to delve deeply into the characters and situations... to "go exploring." I feel that there is a vast canvas on which I'm allowed to paint whatever comes into my mind. But the greatest thing about writing a novel, I think, is that we (like the reader, but more so) get to experience the lives of our characters for months and months as they go through thrilling, dangerous adventures. The characters in our short stories are almost strangers; those in our novels, we grow to love.

EDO VAN BELKOM: What advice would you give to an aspiring horror writer with regard to short story and novel writing?

RICHARD LAYMON: Working on short stories, particularly with proper guidance, is the best way for an aspiring author to learn the basic skills of being a fiction writer. In short stories, the basics are very close to the surface — like the skeleton of a skinny guy. It's easy to know, for instance, whether you've told an actual story or just related an incident. Have you dwelt on irrelevancies? Has your plot gone astray? Was the whole thing botched? With novels, the basics are often hidden under layers of character and story in ways that make them difficult to find. You might go wrong in a novel and not even realize it.

Short stories are also easier to get published than novels. They can provide a means for picking up a few extra bucks. Also, they are very good for helping you break into the field and make a name for yourself. So by all means, write short stories as a way to begin your writing career. But don't focus on short stories to the exclusion of novels. Short stories are like training exercises; the novel is the real game.

———————

Californian Richard Laymon's novels, which include The Cellar, The Beast House, *and* Bite, *have been published in 15 foreign languages. He is also the author of the nonfiction book* A Writer's Tale, *published by Deadline Press, which chronicles his life and career as a horror writer.*

First of all, horror is a genre of emotions, primarily fear, and it's difficult to sustain a constant level of fear over the length of a novel. What you end up with are chapters of build-up, suspense, and payoff, intermingled with other chapters of down time, in which the characters move from one scene to another, contemplate what's happened or what might happen, or try to convince other characters that they are all doomed. As a result, it's hard to sustain a high level of reader interest throughout the entire course of a novel.

A short story, however, usually moves toward just a single fright or moment (a shocking or twist ending perhaps), and when that moment

The following are general story lengths as recognized by professional writers' organizations like the Science Fiction and Fantasy Writers of America and the Horror Writers Association:

0 — 1,500 words
Short-short story

1,500 — 7,500 words
Short story

7,500 — 17,500 words
Novelette

17,500 — 40,000 words
Novella

40,000 words and over
Novel

is reached, there is a satisfactory payoff to the reader as a reward for the time invested in reading the story. The investment of time and attention required to get through a novel is much greater, and the payoff to the reader frequently isn't all that much bigger than the payoff offered by a short story.

The Scenic Route versus the Shortest Distance between Two Points

Novel writers have to reward readers in other ways. Instead of pulling the reader along to get to the ending as quickly as possible, as a writer would do in a short story, they take the reader on a tour through their novel, stopping at points of interest along the way to smell the roses, explore a character, or view some breathtaking vista.

In short stories, every word, every sentence, every event must develop plot or character or atmosphere in some way. There is no room for excess wordage, passive writing, or self-indulgence on the part of the author, and that is why many writers consider short story writing to be more difficult than writing novels.

Think of a short story as a race car trying to get from the start line to the finish line in the shortest amount of time and with the smallest amount of effort possible. And think of a horror novel as a tour bus that wouldn't think anything of stopping by the side of the road for an hour to smell the flowers before loading its passengers back up and trundling on its way once more.

One of the romantic poets (and no, I don't remember which one) once said that a novelist was really just a failed short story writer, and a short story writer was just a failed poet. The point is that the object of writing is to get your message across in as few words as possible.

Novel Ideas versus Short Stories Padded into Novels

If you're unsure whether your idea is meant to be a short story or a novel, you can always let the story determine its own length by starting it without concern for how long it might be when it's finished. Once you're done you can better decide if it can be made into a novel or needs to be trimmed down into a short story.

Many authors write long, then cut down their stories by trimming away all the excess words and scenes. In this way you might start with a first draft of 10,000 words, then cut it down to a tightly written story of 7,000.

I once wrote a story called "Overdue Fines" that, when finished, came in at around 5,000 words. I was unable to sell it until a market listing for a book called *100 Wicked Little Witch Stories* appeared asking for witch stories of no more than 3,000 words. I cut "Overdue Fines" to 3,000 and made a sale. When I related this series of events to horror writer Darrell Schweitzer, a co-editor of the magazine *Weird Tales,* he said, "Then it was never meant to be 5,000 words long." What he meant was that if it worked at 3,000 words, it probably didn't work at 5,000, and didn't need to be that long either.

Cutting stories down usually improves them, but expanding stories into novels isn't always as successful. If you're writing a novel and find yourself short on word count (and let's be realistic about such things, since publishers expect a novel to have a certain heft to it), rather than padding it with more description and extraneous dialogue, think about adding a subplot or two that won't detract from what you've already written but will add some complexity to your storyline.

Writing Horror Comics

If you grew up reading *Tales from the Crypt,* or loved the illustrations in *Weird Tales* as much as you did reading the words, and if you think you'd like to write horror stories for the comics, there are two directions you can take. On the one hand, you can write prose horror fiction with an eye toward getting a foot in the comics-industry door when the opportunity arises. Many horror authors have gone this route, including Joe R. Lansdale, who wrote many issues of *The Preacher* comic series, and Nancy Collins, author of *Sunglasses after Dark,* who penned a long string of *Swamp Thing* comics. Both authors had made a name for themselves in horror, then used their considerable talents to tell stories in the comic-book medium.

On the other hand, some authors have started out in the comics industry, then used that experience to springboard into the novel market. One example is Tim Lucas, whose novel *Throat Sprockets* began life as a comic book and was eventually rewritten as a novel and published by Dell. Another more popular author who took the same route was Neil Gaiman. He first gained fame as the writer behind the *Sandman* series but went on to pen such novels as *Neverwhere* and *Good Omens* (the latter in collaboration with Terry Pratchett).

The writer of a comics issue gives the artist a general overview of the storyline and also indicates how much the story should progress on each page. The writer can also give more detailed instruction to the artist, describing each individual panel. Comics writers must also be good with dialogue, making sure it rings true to character while conveying as much information and emotion as possible in a very limited space.

Writing Horror Screenplays

There's no secret to writing for the movies. The same sort of dogged determination that applies to writing horror novels or short stories applies to writing horror screenplays. The competition level is the same in both mediums, and trying to make your first sale can be just as frustrating whether you're selling novels or screenplays.

One thing is certain, though: if you want to sell to the movies, you should be living in a place where movies are made. That means Hollywood, but a case could be made for New York City, Toronto, or Vancouver. If you live where films are being made, you will be better able to network with filmmakers and eventually might get a screenplay looked at or considered.

If you're not living in Hollywood and have no plans or desire to move there, you'll have to start writing and selling horror stories and novels. Once you've established yourself in the genre, it's only a sideways step into a different medium. Authors like Joe R. Lansdale and Ed Gorman have written several screenplays while living in Texas and Iowa.

Of course, this is general advice, and there are always exceptions to the rule, like Don Mancini who sold his script for the film *Child's Play* while still in film school and has gone on to write and/or produce four films featuring the demon-doll Chucky. And, of course, George A. Romero got his start making horror films in Pittsburgh, Pennsylvania, of all places, where he and a group of friends made *Night of the Living Dead*, one of the scariest horror films of all time.

Writing Horror Poetry

Just about every small press horror magazine publishes horror poetry. It is a terrific way to fill in the gaps and empty white space left at the end of stories or to fill up empty pages between features. Having said that, poetry isn't just filler. Magazines often feature poets in their pages, publishing four to six poems at once along with the poet's bio.

From a writer's standpoint, the best things about horror poetry are that poems generally don't take long to write once their main idea has been conceived, that it's fairly easy to get them published, and that quite often poets can submit and sell several poems at a time. This is a terrific way to build up the number and variety of your publishing credits. However, if you want to sell a novel, you will still have to sell a few pieces of prose fiction to round out your publishing history.

Don't expect to get rich selling horror poetry, though. Most magazines publish poetry in exchange for copies of the magazine the poem appears in, and most poetry collections are self-published, although every once in a while a poet like Bruce Boston reaches a level of prominence in the genre and has a poetry collection published by a small press. One of Boston's more recent poetry collections is *Sensuous Debris,* published by Dark Regions Press. It gathers together more than 50 poems published between 1970 and 1994. As a rule, though, most poets write poetry out of a love for the written word rather than the expectation of any monetary gain.

part two
writing horror

Serious advice for young writers who want to break into the field? The first thing they have to do is read.

— CHARLES L. GRANT

If you're talking about advice to young writers, it's simply to write. Write all the time. The more you write the easier it becomes. [But] it's still hard work. It'll always be hard work.

— MICHAEL McDOWELL

4
what scares you?

Are you afraid of the dark?

In addition to the above question being the title of a popular horror television series for young adults, produced by Nickleodeon, this is a very good thing to ask an aspiring horror writer.

So... are you afraid of the dark? Of things that go bump in the night? If the answer is "yes," that's good, but today's horror genre delves into many other fears. Shadows and things that jump out at you and scream "Boo!" aren't enough any more.

What Are You Afraid Of?

In an article that originally appeared in *Writer's Digest* called "The Horror Writer and the Ten Bears," Stephen King listed his ten greatest fears. Fear of the dark just happens to be King's number one fear, but that's only one of many that have provided the master horror writer with story material over the course of his career.

Here are King's ten greatest fears:

1. Fear of the dark
2. Fear of squishy things
3. Fear of deformity

4. Fear of snakes

5. Fear of rats

6. Fear of closed-in places

7. Fear of insects

8. Fear of death

9. Fear of others

10. Fear for someone else

Obviously King has made use of many of these fears. Number three was used in *Thinner*, while number nine showed up in *Misery*, and number six made an appearance in *Cujo*.

My own list of fears would probably include most of King's, but in a different order. I find number ten — fear for someone else, especially being unable to help someone else in need — to be the strongest of my fears. For example, I often take my young son swimming in a crowded, city-operated swimming pool. He's adventurous and likes to go off on his own, and I try to keep an eye on him, but every once in a while I lose sight of him. Then I begin to panic, searching the crowd for him, imagining he's being held under the water, unable to breath, thrashing wildly, screaming for help while I look for him in vain — And then I find him, happily splashing in the water, and I have to wait for my heart to slow to its normal rhythm.

Fear of death is another of my fears, but I don't so much fear death as I fear dying before my time, before I've had a chance to accomplish something with my life. As a result, many of my stories are about lives being cut short in their prime.

I would be remiss if I didn't mention that fear of rats is a strong fear as well. That fear was the basis of the story "Rat Food," which I co-wrote with David Nickle, and which won the 1997 Bram Stoker Award from the Horror Writers Association.

A good exercise — and a good method for self-evaluation — is to make a list of your own ten greatest fears, being as specific or as general as you like. Once you've done that, come up with a story idea for each of them. At least one of the ideas should make an interesting story. The next obvious step is to start writing — but hold that thought. There are still plenty of things to consider and decisions to be made before you actually begin.

Keeping Track of Your Ideas

Ideas are valuable things to a writer. If you've got too many of them, or at least more ideas than time to turn them all into stories and novels, you might want to write them down in a notebook so you can refer to them later. In my office, I keep a grey notebook with blank lined paper inside it in which I can jot down notes, ideas, and story outlines whenever they come to me. I've also gotten up in the middle of the night on more than one occasion to walk down to the office and make a note of the idea I've just had. I never really want to get out of bed to do this, but I know that if I don't, I will have forgotten the idea by morning and I'll be cursing myself for the rest of the day.

Once the idea is in the notebook, I don't have to write the story until I want to or need to. Sometimes I'll be asked to submit a story to an anthology and I won't have a decent idea. I'll go back to my notebook and pore over the pages and pages of story ideas and outlines until something clicks.

A quick glance through my current notebook reveals a few newspaper article headlines that might someday provide the genesis for a terrific story or two: "Homeless tot killed by pet rat," "Experts 'recondition' man in love with car," and "Boy kills cat for witch's brew." I'll just let your imagination run wild over what might be contained in the articles themselves.

Ideas Are Easy; Stories Are Hard

Many new writers can be guarded about their story ideas, thinking that other writers are predators just waiting to gobble up someone else's idea and claim it as their own. This happens far more in fiction *about* writers than it does in reality. The scenario of two writers, one stealing from the other, makes for great television and stage plays, and it's easily believed by the general public. Sure, it might happen from time to time, and such cases are big news so there's a public perception that it happens all the time, but it does not.

The only case I can recall of an idea being stolen by one writer from another involved Rod Serling, who had heard a would-be writer discussing a story idea. The writer had talked and talked about his idea at countless parties, and when Serling was in need of stories for *The Twilight Zone*, the writer's story came to mind. Serling, thinking the idea was his own, wrote it up. When it was pointed out to him where the story actually came from, Serling realized what he had done, apologized profusely, paid the writer for his story, and gave him the story credit for the episode. After all, no writer wants the reputation of being a thief, and while stealing someone else's idea might work once, it's no way to forge a career.

Still, countless editors have fielded calls and queries from would-be writers explaining that they have some great story ideas. I myself often get calls from people who've got an idea for a book and want to know where they can sell it once it's written. They go on to explain that they don't want to tell me the idea because they're afraid I or someone else might steal it out from under them. Or sometimes they tell me they've got a great idea and would like me to write the story for them. My answer is to ask them to write out their idea fully and give it to me so I can work with it. They never bother.

That's because coming up with ideas, even great ideas, is the easy part. (Remember, Serling's writer talked and talked about his idea but never got around to writing the story.) The hard part is the writing of the story, adding characterization, believable motivation, setting, atmosphere, and a satisfying ending. The old saying that "Art is 1 percent inspiration, and 99 percent perspiration" is a cliché because it's true.

And even if someone else has the same idea as you do, he or she will not necessarily write the same story as you will. I was once asked to provide a story for an anthology called *The Piano Player Has No Fingers*. The idea behind the anthology was for all contributors to write a story with that same title. Of the thirteen stories in the book, no two are alike or even the slightest bit similar.

Good ideas are a valuable commodity, but they are valuable only to a writer who turns them into stories. To paraphrase a saying from the education field, "An idea is a terrible thing to waste." Give the exercise at the end of Sample 1 a try.

Turning an Idea into a Story

Some writers feel that a good idea is more than enough to make a story. Such is not the case, however; an idea alone ends up being what is called a H.A.I.T.E. story.

Here's An Idea, The End.

I'm an idea writer. Everything of mine is permeated with my love of ideas — both big and small. It doesn't matter what it is as long as it grabs me, and holds me, and fascinates me.

— RAY BRADBURY

sample 1
ten rapid-fire story ideas

Ideas are easy to come by, but turning them into stories is hard. If you don't believe it, try coming up with a number of story ideas in rapid succession. Write them all down, no matter what you think of them at the time, and stop when you've got ten or so ideas. Of course, not all of them will be gems, but at least one of them might be worth turning into a story, and perhaps even more than one. The point is that real writers don't suffer from writer's block, but instead find they never have enough time to write all the things they want to. There's no such thing as writer's block — and no room for it in a professional writer's life (if you don't write, you don't eat) — only a lack of will and determination.

Now, let's see what we can come up with.

On our mark.

Get set.

Go!

1. An obscure book in the local library is checked out by a middle-aged woman, who later dies under mysterious circumstances. A check reveals that the last four people who have taken the book out in the last 20 years have also died mysteriously.

2. A television film crew arrives at the house of an old woman wanting to interview her for a documentary they are doing on a satanic cult they say she belongs to. She insists she's not a member of any cult, but they carry on filming the documentary just the same.

3. A fisherman notices his nets are less and less full with each month and he can't figure out why. Then one day his nets suddenly seem full to bursting, and he eagerly hauls them in only to find he's caught just one fish, a huge, monstrous creature that has obviously been eating his usual catch.

4. A talk show host wants to defraud a so-called mentalist on his show, but what he doesn't realize is that the mentalist's powers are actually real and he uses them to turn the tables on the host.

5. A young boy wants nothing more than to be a member of the Marauders gang. They agree to let him join, and he's overjoyed. But before he can be a full member, he has to do something really bad. (I'll leave the bad part to your imagination.)

6. A family of werewolves chance across an abandoned baby in the forest. They decide to take it in and raise it as one of their own. What they don't know is that the child is the result of a vicious rape and the mother wanted nothing to do with the child, instinctively knowing that the baby will turn out worse and more evil than its father. The wolves raise the child, then introduce him to human society (as they believe is right), where he becomes a violent predator. Now the werewolf family must find and catch him before he kills again.

7. A vampire who has adjusted well to life among humans hears a knock at his door. It's a young woman, a goth, who says, "Take me in. I want to be like you. Make me like you." He laughs, not knowing what she's talking about, but while he's laughing she slits her wrist and the blood begins to pour out of her arm. Having no other choice the vampire takes her inside, sucks at her wound, and nurses her back to health.

8. An avenging angel comes to Earth and attends a white-supremacist rally in the woods in the Deep South. The angel has been sent to start righting the wrongs of society, and he decides to begin with the most vocal of the men on the platform speaking to the congregation. With nothing more than a sweep of an arm and a flick of the wrist, the angel has taken the man and put him in the body of a black man, on stage in the midst of all his former cohorts. Maybe the angel transforms him back to see if he might change his point of view; maybe he doesn't.

9. A serial killer is dying of cancer, and although he's never been caught, never even suspected by police, he is haunted by the ghosts of his victims, which turns out to be far more terrifying than any punishment he could have ever received from the authorities. His only consolation is that he will be dead soon and probably in hell, which can't be any worse than what he's going through at the moment — or so he thinks.

10. The body of a usually modest and conservative young woman is invaded by a demon spirit that forces her to do things that she never would have dreamed she was capable of doing. The demon remains for a few weeks before moving on, but when it does finally leave, the young woman finds that she enjoyed her misdeeds and wants for them to continue, demon or no.

Done. Now, all that took just under a half-hour and produced a few decent story ideas. How did you do?

EXERCISE

Take a half-hour and jot down whatever ideas pop into your head, no matter how silly or bizarre. If you don't like the results, try combining the ideas from more than one story.

So how does one go about turning a good idea into a story? Stories need characters and settings and problems and solutions in order to be complete. An idea is only the starting point. Take, for example, my story "The Piano Player Has No Fingers." I was given the title, and that was also the idea — a piano player with no fingers. Since I was writing the story shortly after the 1992 Winter Olympics, my first idea was to write a story about two rival piano players, one of whom paid someone else to break the fingers (or even cut them off) of his rival, a la Tonya Harding and Nancy Kerrigan. I started the story but before long realized that it wasn't going anywhere. So I stopped writing and resumed thinking.

My second idea was better. Much better.

(Spoiler Warning: Anyone who doesn't want to know how the story ends should go directly to the next section.)

I came up with the idea of a piano with human fingers in place of the keys. A great idea, but not much of a story. I needed all the other things — the hard stuff — to turn the idea into a story.

I decided to make it a mystery, with one Detective Joe Williams investigating the Piano Player Murders, in which the top piano players in the city have been killed and their fingers cut off. Detective Williams goes to the house of Lawrence Hayden, a wealthy music expert and amateur musician, who has an extensive musical instrument collection and who writes a music column for the local paper. The detective asks Hayden questions about the murders, hoping Hayden might have some new ideas on this very perplexing case. Williams gets little information, but Hayden comes across as the bad guy. After Williams leaves, Hayden, angered by the intrusion, goes off to his private music room, where the piano is kept. In seclusion, Hayden begins to play the favorite of all his rare and exotic instruments.

Fortunately, the finished story was equal to the quality of the idea, and "The Piano Player Has No Fingers" ended up being a finalist for the Arthur Ellis Award for Best Crime Short Story (presented by the Crime Writers of Canada) of the year. Not all good ideas end up being good stories, but you'll never know for sure until you write them.

Writing What You Know

Even if you have only a mild or passing interest in creative writing, you've probably heard the expression "Write what you know." Sounds simple enough, but what does it mean?

It means that you should write about things with which you are familiar. If you're a parent, writing what you know would include stories about parents coping with life while they raise their children and try to make something of their own careers. Or if you live in a small town in the middle of nowhere, it might be a good idea to set your stories in a small town in the middle of nowhere. By doing this, you won't have to struggle to get the details right and your work will be better for it.

Some writers have taken the "write what you know" maxim literally and have created fictional characters based on their own lives and experiences. Two examples are mystery writers Alison Gordon and Kathy Reichs. For five years Gordon covered the Toronto Blue Jays for the *Toronto Star*; in her series of mystery novels, her main character, Kate Henry, covers the Toronto Titans for the *Planet,* while solving murders in her spare time. Kathy Reichs is a forensic anthropologist who works for the Quebec government; her heroine is Tempe Brennan, a forensic anthropologist who works for the Quebec government.

A Few Words With...

Ed Gorman

on crossing horror with other genres

EDO VAN BELKOM: You began your career writing mysteries. How did you begin to delve into horror?

ED GORMAN: I grew up reading as much science fiction and horror as I did mysteries. That's why I suppose I consider myself a writer rather than a "mystery writer" or "horror writer." I also write westerns and love those too.

EDO VAN BELKOM: What special talents does a horror writer need that a mystery, romance, or science fiction writer doesn't?

ED GORMAN: The ability to contact your most primal fears. *The Shrinking Man* is, for me, about impotence in all senses. *I Am Legend* is about isolation and loneliness, the ultimate statement of the outsider. *Christine* is about the obsessions (maybe even psychoses) that the outsider uses to compensate for feeling neglected and scorned. In my own writing, I've only once been able to contact my primal fear, in a book called *Cage of Night*, which for me is about how a beautiful young girl uses the love of young men to destroy not only them but herself as well. In a way, me being one of the young men, it's the most auto-biographical novel I've ever written. And I think that's why it's the only one of my six or seven horror novels that is completely successful as a terror tale and a social observation.

EDO VAN BELKOM: What is it about the horror genre that allows it to be so easily combined with other genres?

ED GORMAN: To me, all popular fiction is the same. Elmore Leonard's westerns are almost always pure suspense stories set in the west; most of Stephen King's horror novels are mainstream novels of character with one supernatural element put into the mix, and this is especially true of the brilliant *The Green Mile*; Ramsey Campbell writes John O'Hara–style character studies about people caught in the dark world. Hell, look at Ed McBain's *Ghosts*, a truly creepy (and sexy) police procedural. As Howard Hawks, the director, once said, "All good stories are about character and action. Period." That's true for *The Searchers, Psycho, Alien,* and *8½*. It just depends on what colors you choose to hue your tale with. But the basic elements — and the building blocks — are essentially the same. At least as I see it.

Ed Gorman is the author of several highly regarded horror novels, including Cage of Night, Black River Falls, *and* Daughter of Darkness. *He is also an accomplished author of mystery, science fiction, young adult, and western novels, as well as a countless number of short stories.*

Unfortunately, not all of us have such interesting jobs. For that reason, writing about what you know doesn't mean writing about yourself. If you are a plumber or a teacher, you don't have to write stories about plumbers and teachers. You could, however, write stories about average, working-class people who have extraordinary events happen in their lives, or about teenage kids trying to grow up while dealing with school, peer pressure, and family problems.

Writing what you know is more about the sort of emotions with which you're familiar than the actual events that occur in your life. If it wasn't, most of my stories would be about a bearded, almost-40-year-old family man who spends most of his time sitting in front of a computer screen.

Writing What You Don't Know: Research

But what happens when you want to — or have to — write about a subject of which you know absolutely nothing?

It's called research.

Before you groan and roll your eyes at the prospect of reading stuffy old books in hopes of finding what you need, be aware that there are plenty of different kinds of research. Luckily, doing research for horror stories isn't as in-depth as it is for, say, science fiction or police procedurals. Making a horror story ring true — and that's all you're shooting for, the appearance of it being a story that could actually happen — doesn't take more than a few well-placed facts or details.

To make my collector of rare musical instruments in "The Piano Player Has No Fingers" sound believable, I had to do a little research into rare and exotic musical instruments. I picked up a few names — clavichord, harpsichord, and perhaps a few others — and found pictures of them all so I would know what these instruments looked like. Then I proceeded to mention them in the story, not worrying if I got a name wrong here or there — even calling one instrument "a strangely twisted horn instrument with a complicated valve system" — because my detective, the point-of-view character, didn't have to know the names of the instruments either. Later, when I needed a few details about a single instrument, I took a brief description from the cutline of a photo in a book and used it almost word for word. The result was an entirely plausible scenario.

I had to do more firsthand research when I was writing my story "Ice Bridge." I remembered reading an article about truck loggers in British Columbia — truckers who drive huge, log-laden trucks over frozen lakes in winter to save time when bringing their loads to the mill. I thought the situation would make for a great adventure story, but 30 years had passed since I'd read the article in the *Toronto Star* and I was unable to find it in the archives of my local library. I decided to talk with some trucking people in the hope they could give me some information. I called the Ontario Trucking Association, who passed me on to the Northern Ontario Trucking Association, who passed me on to the British Columbia Trucking Association, who passed me on to the Interior British Columbia Trucking Association (I know I'm probably making mistakes on the names of these fine groups, but research isn't crucial on this point), who finally passed me on to the *Prince George Citizen* and the forestry reporter there — Kent Bernsohn. I spoke with him for about an hour, telling him the plot of my story and asking him about certain things I needed to know for my plot to work. He answered all my questions and even gave me a few details that would make my story better. (One thing in the writer's favor is that people love talking about themselves and are always flattered when you find what they do for a living interesting.) I included everything he told me in the story, and it turned out to be one of my best.

A coda to this episode: After reading "Ice Bridge," the editor of *Truck News,* John G. Smith, asked me to write a monthly serial about a truck driver for his newspaper. One of the reasons Smith approached me for the job was that all my trucking details in "Ice Bridge" were spot on. "Mark Dalton: Owner/Operator" has been continuously published in monthly installments since June 1999.

Knowing Where You're Going: Outlining

Now that you know what you'd like to write and you've done all the research you're going to need to complete the story, it might be time to write up an outline so you'll have a rough idea of what should happen in your story. There are several benefits to outlining your stories and novels, especially in the horror genre:

- Because the success of your story depends so much on its ending, it's a great help to know exactly where your story needs to go so you'll know just what to do to get it there. A good analogy is that of making a trip across town: you'd want to know the route you'd be taking.

- Knowing how the story will end helps you set up that ending to make it satisfying to the reader. If I hadn't known how my story "The Piano Player Has No Fingers" was going to end, I wouldn't have known how many murders needed to be committed, nor would I have spent as much time setting up Lawrence Hayden's character to make him a believable villain. But because I knew exactly where the story was going, everything fell into place instead of falling apart.

- Of course, all the elements leading up to the ending can be written into the story or novel after you've finished the first draft, but that's far more work than including them the first time through. And quite often the element you want to insert doesn't easily fit into a scene, and you have to write far more than you'd planned just to include some bit of information.

By making an outline, you're doing more work before you actually start writing, but far less work after you've written the story. This is especially helpful in the case of novels, because inserting something after the fact means you must go through the entire book to make sure that all the references are consistent. Whenever I've outlined a novel, I've included every scene in the book. As a result, the outline might run 10,000 to 15,000 words and incorporate 60 to 80 scenes. That way any holes or problems with the plot will be discovered early on and can be easily fixed, making the actual writing of the novel the most enjoyable part of its creation.

Of course, there are also some benefits to be had by not outlining, and some writers seem to prefer working this way. Many authors are vehemently opposed to any sort of outlining at all. They may make a few notes about events or characters in their stories and novels, but that is the extent of their preparation. Their argument is that if they knew how everything was going to turn out, there would be no reason for them to actually write the book. The benefit of not outlining is that the story can take some very unexpected turns: if even the author doesn't know where the story is going, how can the reader?

Working this way makes the writing of a story or novel more adventure than work, and these authors enjoy discovering where the story takes them. When it works well, the characters can take on a life of their own, surprising both the author and the eventual reader. When it doesn't work, storylines end up at dead ends, and a rewrite — or a lot of thought — is required before the story can continue.

If you're unsure which method is best for you, experiment with a few outlines, then write a story or two without one just to see which is a better fit.

I have written stories both ways. For the last five years I've liked having my stories completely outlined, even to the point where key dialogue is included. That has given my stories a tightness and a characteristic twist ending. More recently, however, I've had some good ideas that were incomplete — good beginnings without middles or ends. I just started writing the stories with what I had, hoping that an ending would come to me. Sometimes something better did occur to me, but at other times a story might sit for months until I figured out what to do with it. Both methods worked out in the end, but it's impossible to say which one would suit an individual writer best. Like most other things in writing, there's no better substitute than trial and error, and in the case of horror writing, trial and terror.

Take a look at Sample 2, an outline for a story called "Rock and Rollers Never Die." This was my first idea for the story, but it seemed a little too predictable to spend any time writing it. (Although reading it again for inclusion in this book, it doesn't seem like too bad an idea and I just might write this story yet.) However, when I was asked to come up with a erotic story involving a demon for the anthology *Demon Sex*, I decided I'd use this basic storyline but change it slightly to better suit the anthology. I decided to have the reporter trying to figure out how a decrepit, aging rock star could still make young girls scream in the aisles. Through her efforts, the reporter finds out that the rock star has a sort of hypnotic or telepathic ability and can manipulate his audience to lust after him — even through his recorded music. When she discovers this, he uses his powers to make her want him desperately, even though his physical appearance is absolutely revolting to her.

It's a different story than the one in the outline, but it nevertheless began with the idea outlined in "Rock and Rollers Never Die."

outline: Rock and Rollers never die

A pushy reporter is looking for a big story to get her back on top. She decides to do an in-depth story on a long-time rock and roll star. She wants to find out what keeps him going as the guy is seriously old — a character modeled after Keith Richards of the Rolling Stones.

What drives him after 35 years in the business? There have been rumors of drugs, alcohol, even New Age channeling. She decides to find out.

She poses as a groupie, dresses provocatively and hangs out by the back door before the concert because she's heard he often picks up girls before his shows. It works and he ends up taking her into his dressing room. Before the concert they have sex — she really goes out of her way to please him — but he leaves to go onstage before either of them are satisfied.

After a few songs he comes backstage again, has sex again, but does not allow himself to climax.

He goes back out on stage leaving her feeling more and more tired, drained. She realizes that he's using their sexual energy to put on his show. She wants to stop him before she gets hurt, but she's too weak and powerless to do anything to fight back.

He returns for more when the concert is over. She can hear the crowd roaring just outside the door. They've been cheering wildly all night.

They have sex again. This time he brings her to orgasm in a powerful, body-shuddering climax, then goes out for his encore, full of energy.

Refreshed.

She falls asleep, totally wiped out, unable to move.

She wakes up later, how much later she doesn't know. The room is empty, dark. She can hardly move.

She bolsters herself with the knowledge that as wild as it might be, at least she has her story.

Finally she gets up, goes over to a mirror and sees her body and face are withered and old, like that of a hag. Her life force has literally been sucked from her body.

She begins to cry.

She has her story, but no one will ever believe her.

5
elements of horror: the blood and guts

Getting Started: Story Introductions

In many ways, the beginning of your story or novel is its most important part. The beginning is your chance to hook the reader into reading more, and that chance won't last longer than a few seconds — the amount of time it will take someone to read the first few lines of your story.

Most aspiring writers don't know where to begin their stories. Many of the student stories I've read over the years actually begin on about page five. In those five pages the story's character is rolling out of bed, having breakfast or some other boring thing, and is not confronted by a problem until several pages (and several hundred words) later. But stories must get rolling almost immediately, and learning how to do that will save you from receiving dozens of rejection slips over the years.

How do you hook the reader with just a few words to make certain that he or she will want to read on to find out what happens next? There are fundamentally five ways to start a story or novel, and each one requires a certain talent.

Description

Everyone has heard the line "It was a dark and stormy night." It has become a cliché, an overused phrase that means nothing anymore. At one time, however, "It was a dark and stormy night" was an effective descriptive opening, creating an atmosphere and painting a picture of an evening on which it might be best to stay indoors.

But while "a dark and stormy night" has become old hat, the principle behind it hasn't. Describing the setting of your story is still one of the most effective ways to begin a tale, even though it is at the same time one of the most difficult to do successfully. Unfortunately, a simple description of a place and time can be rather boring, unless you make your writing fresh and alive.

One of the best authors of descriptive openings is Ray Bradbury. His prose style, which is sometimes rather poetic and even baroque, is perfect for description that sets the stage for the story. My favorite example is the opening to Bradbury's classic novel, *Something Wicked This Way Comes*:

> *First of all, it was October, a rare month for boys. Not that all months aren't rare. But there be bad and good, as the pirates say. Take September, a bad month: school begins. Consider August, a good month: school hasn't begun yet. July, well, July's really fine: there's no chance in the world for school. June, no doubting it, June's best of all, for the school doors spring wide and September's a billion years away.*

This description continues for a few more paragraphs until he gets to October (one of Bradbury's favorite months) and how Halloween came early that year. Obviously the poetry and imagery of the language carry the passage, since all that is being described here is the time of year. It is enjoyable to read, but the sunny lines slowly darken until the opening's final line:

> *And that was the October week when they grew up overnight, and were never so young anymore...*

How could you not want to read on and find out about what happened to the two young boys when one of the most extraordinary carnivals stops in their town?

Character

Starting a story with the description of a character is very similar to starting it with straight description. In the Bradbury example, what was described was the time of year (and along the way, a bit about the town and the two main characters of the story), but when you start with a character, your material is far more limited.

Obviously, then, the character with which you begin should be the most interesting one in the story. It doesn't have to be the main character, or the hero, but there should be something very peculiar or unique about the character.

A great example of starting with a character can be found in the cult horror novel *Big Gurl*, by Thom Metzger and Richard P. Scott. *Big Gurl* is about Mary Cup, a queen-sized package of beauty and brawn who is disconnected from reality and is just as comfortable with killing people as she is with playing with her dolls. Obviously, a description of her character is a prime candidate for the opening of the novel, and authors Metzger and Scott deliver:

> *Mary Cup sat waist-deep in a pool of mud behind her house, swaying from side to side and flailing her arms above her head. Her fists were filled with dozens of wriggling worms. She began to pound her heels into the mud in a steady rhythm, slowly at first, then faster and faster. Suddenly she stopped and held the worms to her ears like a set of headphones.*
>
> *"Code Blue — Code Blue. Top-secret transmit on frequency Double-Seven Niner. Prepare to receive scramble message." She twisted her hands, grinding the worms into her ears...*

It's evident that Mary Cup isn't any normal little girl. She's *Big Gurl*, and this introduction promises that the novel will be something quite different.

It does not disappoint.

Dialogue

Have you ever been riding on the bus or on the subway, and for lack of anything better to do, started listening in on other people's conversations? The problem is that you've begun listening in the middle of the conversation and you've missed all the background information that would help you make sense of what's being said. As a result, you're wondering, "What are they talking about?" and you're almost tempted to stay on the bus past your stop just to find out what's going on.

The same hook works for story openings. Starting your story in the middle of a conversation grabs a reader's attention, making the reader want to read on to find out what happens next.

Dialogue is a doubly effective way to capture a reader's interest because of the ease with which it provides information to the reader. A general rule in writing is that three lines of dialogue are worth three pages of exposition. That sounds somewhat simplistic, but it is an effective way of explaining how much information can be brought into the story through dialogue.

Richard Laymon's novel *Out Are the Lights* starts with dialogue, and even though few words are said, there are all sorts of interesting bits contained therein:

> *"You sure it's not haunted?" Ray asked.*
>
> *The weathered Victorian House cast a shadow over its weedy yard and Ray's Trans-Am.*
>
> *"Wouldn't that be rich," Tina said. "I've never seen a ghost."*
>
> *"This may be your big opportunity."*

Take the first line, " 'You sure it's not haunted?' Ray asked." From this we can surmise that a group of people are approaching a haunted house. They're unsure of what they might find inside, but there have been stories about it being haunted, perhaps by ghosts. We also get some characterization from these few lines. Ray is a bit frightened, needing reassurance, while Tina is self-confident, considering it all fun and looking forward to a good scare. So too is the reader, who reads on to see if Tina gets her wish, as the teens plan to stay in the house overnight.

Action

Action is probably the easiest and best way to start a story or novel. Action is exciting. Characters involved in action are interesting. Usually, the greater and more intense the action, the more interest it generates within the reader, but that's not always the case.

Jack Ketchum's excellent first novel, *Off Season*, starts with a scene of intense action in which a woman who had stopped to help a little girl stumbling by the road ends up being chased through the forest, literally running for her life. The scene ends with the woman getting free of her pursuers and leaping off a cliff into the cold, churning waves of the ocean. It is an intense opening and draws the reader into a novel that remains just as intense throughout its 180 pages.

However, action doesn't always have to be so over-the-top exciting. For example, my short story "Mark of the Beast" opens with very little action, but the action is just creepy enough to get the story on its way.

> *The cabin's silence was broken only by the sound of the rocking chair's runners as they cut into the cold hardwood floor.*
>
> *Nadia Varga sat in the rocker, a knitted shawl covering her shoulders, a flannel blanket over her legs, and a two-shot, double-barreled shotgun sitting across her lap.*
>
> *She was waiting for the beast.*
>
> *And when it came, she was going to kill it.*

If the actual beginning of your story is not long on action, you might consider moving an action scene from the end of the tale to the beginning. Once you've got the reader interested, you can begin telling the story of what led up to that first scene. It is a tried and true method, most commonly found in mystery stories and novels.

Letters and diaries (epistolary format)

An epistolary novel is one written in the form of letters. The most famous epistolary novel is the classic *Dracula*, by Bram Stoker, which begins with entries from Jonathan Harker's journal and is sprinkled throughout with diary entries, letters, and telegrams sent to and from the various characters. For many years, this was the most popular way to write a novel. It is woefully outdated now, though there have been updated versions featuring e-mail messages.

However, the epistolary format is an excellent device for starting stories and novels. A letter can provide the reader with a lot of background information. The letter brings the person receiving the letter, as well as the reader, up to speed before the story begins.

Richard Laymon uses this format to begin his novel *The Beast House*, which is a sequel to his bestselling debut novel, *The Cellar*. The first letter is from Janice Crogan to bestselling writer Gorman Hardy, informing him of the history of the Beast House (the house from *The Cellar*) and telling him about a diary kept by Lilly Thorn (an occupant of the house at the turn of the century). The letter ends with a P.S.:

> P.S. This thing here makes your ghost from Black River Falls look like a sissy.

Enough to grab a reader's attention? Perhaps, but if it isn't, Laymon also includes a page from the diary, Gorman Hardy's response, and a few more letters, all of which ultimately bring the writer (and reader) to Malcasa Point, California, the setting for the novel.

Another very effective use of the epistolary format to open a novel can be found in Jeff Rice's excellent vampire novel, *The Night Stalker*. The book, written by Rice (a newspaper reporter in real life, but acting as a advertising man/producer in the book), reports on the events experienced by newspaper reporter Karl Kolchak while covering a string of murders in Las Vegas. The novel begins with a letter from Kolchak to Rice, explaining all that happened and asking Rice if he might want to help him get the true story told.

Finally, another variation on the epistolary format uses a newspaper advertisement, warning sign, or official transcript to get things started. Stephen King's first novel, *Carrie,* starts off this way, with a news item from the Westover, Maine, weekly *Enquirer,* August 19, 1966, which reports that a freak rain of stones fell out of a clear blue sky onto the house of Mrs. Margaret White, causing considerable damage to her roof. It is an innocuous little article, until it mentions that Margaret White lives with her daughter, Carrietta. Here is our first introduction to the Carrie of the title, so as the book begins we know that strange things happen around her. Since she was only three at the time of the incident related in the newspaper, stranger things are likelier still to happen. This story beginning is especially effective because the entire novel is sprinkled with similar bits of information, and although King admits that they were originally an attempt to give the novel a length more suitable to the demands of the publishing world, it actually gives the story more impact and edges it with terror.

As effective as this format can be, it really only puts off starting your story or novel by the more conventional methods of description, character, action, and dialogue. However, by the time you must introduce these things, you've hooked your reader, who might then be more forgiving if and when your story begins to lose some steam.

For some practice on creating effective openings, see Sample 3.

Creating Atmosphere: Setting the Stage

Atmosphere is likely more important in horror than in any other genre. Sure, romance novels might need the rain to fall or the sun to shine to give added weight and significance to the heroine's inner mood, but in the horror genre, atmosphere sometimes permeates entire novels. In some works of quiet horror, atmosphere is part of a book's terror.

Fortunately, atmosphere is rather easy to create in prose fiction. Feelings of tension, suspense, and horror can be caused two different ways: by what you write about, and by how it is written.

What you write

The easiest way to create atmosphere is through what you write about, especially if you remain aware of your senses. You may just be writing something on paper, but that doesn't mean that all five of your senses can't be involved in the experience.

Say you're trying to create an atmosphere of creepiness along a long deserted stretch of country road that you have to walk to get home. First of all, you could use your sense of sight and make it a dark night, and perhaps there is a full moon out, causing scraggly shadows from the trees to cut across the road. Next your sense of touch comes into play, as the dirt and stones of the road are pushing like so many dull spikes through the bottoms of your soft-soled shoes, and your heart is pounding as if it might burst with fear at any moment. Then bring in a smell, like the fresh scent of the day being gone and replaced with the smell of something dead and rotting wafting toward you from somewhere up the road. Taste comes next, as the fear of what's ahead of you makes the bile build up at the back of your throat, causing you to gag.

sample 3
story openings

There are five ways to begin a piece of fiction. The following are examples of the five different techniques (Description, Character, Action, Dialogue, and Epistolary), each used to begin a story about three kids approaching an old house, on a deserted street — a house reputed to be haunted by the ghost of murder victims who were killed there 20 years previously.

Description

The Old House sat at the top of a lump of a hill, leaning to one side as if it might topple over and roll down the street if the wind blew strongly enough. One of the two windows on the top floor had been smashed by rocks, and it made the front of the house look like a face — an old, haggard face that had lost an eye. The front door had been kicked in too, then boarded up, making it look like the toothless mouth of an old, ugly hag.

Character

Sandra didn't want to go for an explore in the Manson house, and I didn't exactly blame her. I felt scared about going into that old, rotting corpse of a building too, but I couldn't admit it. Sandra was a girl, and it was all right for her to be afraid of old houses, noises in the night, and spiders, but I was almost 12 and the oldest in the group and I couldn't let anyone know I was scared, even if it killed me.

Action

They approached the house with slow cautious steps, as if they were walking across an old creaky floor and not the front lawn of the Manson house. Billy, in the lead, moved behind one of the gnarled elms out front and stopped to look at the house now that they were closer. It was spooky all right, but they'd said they'd spend the night inside and he was bound to make sure they went through with it.

Suddenly a scream sliced the stillness. It was Sandra.

Billy turned in time to see the dog bounding up the drive toward them, spikes in the collar around its neck, sharp fangs glinting in the moonlight, and an angry fire alight in its eyes.

"Inside the house," Billy cried.

"No..." whined Sandra. "I can't."

"We have to. It's our only chance."

Dialogue
"Do you think it's haunted?" asked Sandra.

"Course it's haunted," said Billy. "Didn't you read the newspaper? Old man Manson killed his two kids and wife inside there 20 years ago. They found the three of them, but Manson slipped away."

"You don't think he's in there, do you?"

"He might be," said Billy. "Why else would he let the place get so run down?"

Sandra shrugged.

"To make it look like no one lives there anymore, that's why."

She looked at him, a terrified look in her eyes.

Billy laughed. "C'mon, let's go. This is going to be cool!"

Epistolary

Manson family found dead
Chas Manson wanted by Police

Police were called last night to the Manson home at 32 Frederic Road after a neighbor noticed a door left open in the wind. Upon investigation three bodies were discovered lying in the living room of the home.

Marilyn Manson and her two sons, Chip and Dale, were found with multiple stab wounds in the chest and back in what Shadoe County Sheriff Buford Griffin called "The worst act of violence I've seen in my 23 years in law enforcement."

Sheriff's deputies spent much of the night searching the neighboring countryside for Chas Manson, who is wanted for questioning in the murders.

Billy crumpled the photocopy of the newspaper article in his hand and motioned to Sandra that it was time to head inside the old Manson house.

"Why do we have to go in there?" she asked, not for the first time that night.

"Just for the hell of it," answered Billy.

For the hell of it, indeed.

EXERCISE

Take a story you've written, or an idea you have for a story, and write several different beginnings to it. Chances are you'll find one you like, and you'll be well on your way to finishing a story with a top-flight beginning.

Then comes your sense of hearing, with the soft whisper of midnight wind through the trees, the scrape of your shoes over the road, the snap of a twig in the woods on your right, and a low throaty moan of pain coming at you out of the darkness, calling for you and telling you *not* to be afraid.

Of course you don't have to use all five senses for every scene in which you want to create some atmosphere, but you should keep in mind that they are there if and when you need them.

How you write

The five senses can be a great tool in creating atmosphere in a horror story or novel, but you won't always want to spend time describing the weather, your character's heart rate, the noise going on in the background, or the taste of your character's own body fluids as they move out of their usual places. Sometimes the senses aren't even a factor. What if your character is stuck in a room that is completely dark? After you've said it's dark, what then? When these factors come into play, it's time to flex your writing muscle and create tension by the *way* in which you write a scene.

There are two basic ways in which you can create tension through writing style: by writing short and by writing long.

Writing short paragraphs and sentences and using short words can do wonders to create urgency in your story. It's an excellent device for building suspense, particularly when a lot of exciting action is happening.

The following is an excerpt from my short story "Ice Bridge." At this point in the story, a truck-logger is driving his log-laden truck across a frozen lake and is desperately trying to outdrive a pressure crack that has formed under his truck. He must reach shore before the crack gets any bigger and causes him and his truck to fall through the ice.

> He firmed up his foot on the gas pedal and stood on it with all his weight.

> The engine began to strain as the speedometer inched past 70.... He remained on the pedal, knowing he'd be across in less than a minute.

> The sound grew louder, changing from a crunching, cracking sound to something resembling a gunshot.

He looked down.

The crack in front of the truck had grown bigger, firing out in front of him in all directions like the scraggly branches of a December birch.

"C'mon, c'mon," he said pressing his foot harder on the gas even though it was a wasted effort. The pedal was already down as far as it would go.

Then suddenly the cracking sound grew faint, as if it had been dampened by a splash of water.

A moment later, crunching again.

Cracking.

He looked up. The shoreline was a few hundred metres away. In a few seconds there would be solid ice under his wheels and then nothing but wonderful, glorious, hard-packed frozen ground.

The shortness of the paragraphs and sentences whisks you along, and the pace at which you're reading is the same pace at which the action takes place in the story.

Doing the opposite — writing long paragraphs and sentences and using longer words — can also be a useful tool in setting up a big scare. You've seen horror movies in which prior to a big fright, the characters are involved in some inane patter about nothing in particular. Just when you, the viewer, have relaxed, thinking nothing's going to happen, you're hit with the severed head falling out of a closet, or the cat jumping into the frame, terrifying the otherwise brave heroine.

You can achieve the same effect in prose fiction. Including a few paragraphs of somewhat boring talk or description is a great way to get your readers to lower their defenses so that when you say "Boo!" you have a good chance of giving them a scare.

This excerpt is from my short story "No Kids Allowed." A husband and wife are taking care of their nieces, even though their landlord doesn't allow any children in his building — period. The reason he doesn't allow them is because he's a ghoul who steals children's life force so that he can live forever. But he's tired of living and wants to grow old and die; therefore, No Kids Allowed.

"I'll see them to bed if you clean up in here," Mary said, her right eyebrow arched highly and her lips curled in a sly half-smile. "Maybe we can rendezvous back here in say... ten minutes?"

"Sounds good to me," Alex said. He collected the glasses and bowls from the living room table while the twins were in the bathroom brushing their teeth. Later, as he was wiping the table with a damp cloth, he could hear Mary's voice coming from the bedroom. Probably reading the girls a bedtime story.

He could also hear something at the door. It was the same muted cry that he'd heard that morning, but now there was something added to it. A scratching sound — as if the dog had returned and wanted to come inside.

Alex crept silently up to the door. The sound grew louder as he neared until there could be no mistaking that there was indeed a dog on the other side.

Remembering that the snicking of the locks had scared the dog away the first time, Alex crouched down to look under the door, hoping to see a paw or some fur through the crack. He was down on all fours when he finally had his head sideways against the carpet and could see through the tiny crack between the door and the floor.

The lights of the hallway produced an unbroken band of white under the door.

There was no dog out in the hall.

Suddenly, the door exploded inward. Something heavy landed on top of Alex and was gone. He had to gasp for air. Several ribs had been cracked and there was a searing, white-hot pain knifing across his midsection.

In the first couple of paragraphs, Mary and Alex are putting the kids to bed. How boring. They hint of possibly having sex later, then Alex is wiping the table. And then he notices something and there is a slow build-up toward — BOO! — all hell breaking loose as the ghoul breaks in looking for the children.

Characters: People to Believe In

Good characterization is crucial to the success of every short story or novel. Read the book review section of your weekend paper or favorite monthly magazine and you'll find countless instances of lack of characterization cited as the reason a book has failed.

But what does that mean, exactly?

It means making the characters in your story or novel seem like real living people. If your story has a father in it, that father must seem like a real father, caring about his kids, working hard to support his family, and doing all the things that make men fathers. If you've got children or teenagers in your story, you must understand the way they speak and get that right, using all the slang and phrases popular among the kids their age. You have to know what interests kids that age and how they interact with other kids and with their parents. If you've got a neighborhood cop in your story, then you've got to make him act like a cop; and not like a cop you've seen on television or in the movies but like a neighborhood cop acts as he's patrolling his area. Good characterization is in the details we give the reader about the character.

In "Rat Food," the story for which David Nickle and I won the Bram Stoker Award, the characterization of the old woman in the story, Mrs. Puhn, is crucial to the success of the piece. Not only is she an old woman, she is also slowly losing her mind, confusing the rats in her home with her long-lost cat, Sweetie. But the characterization doesn't end there. She's also afraid of being taken out of her home like the other women along the street have been, and she's distrustful of her daughter, whom she sees as an enemy, because her daughter is likely to be the one who will send her to a home.

All this information can't be conveyed in just a short time. Rather, it must be given to the reader slowly, each bit building upon the next until a fully fleshed-out character emerges.

In this excerpt from the beginning of the story, Mrs. Puhn has just been startled by a rat in her kitchen and has fallen down.

> She rolled onto her stomach, hoping she wouldn't roll onto a piece of broken glass or get her dress too dirty with jam. It was a white dress and Patty had washed it the last time she'd been by. Was that last week or earlier? Mrs. Puhn wasn't sure. Just last

The personages in a tale shall be alive, except in the case of corpses, and always the reader shall be able to tell the corpses from the others.

— MARK TWAIN

week, she decided. Patty went to the pharmacy to refill my pre-scription — and there's ten pills left in the container.

Patty was Mrs. Puhn's only child and her only companion since all of her other friends had left the neighborhood. They'd all gone to "Retirement Homes" and hospitals, where their children had convinced them they'd be better taken care of.

But Mrs. Puhn would have none of that. This is my home, she'd say. I've lived here all my life. What would I do anywhere else?

Her next-door neighbor, Mrs. Franklin, had put up the same argument. But she eventually gave in to the pressures of family and "friends," and moved out last fall. Mrs. Puhn had watched her leave from the living room window, too terrified even to step out onto the stoop and tell her old friend goodbye.

Patty hadn't been too insistent that Mrs. Puhn join Mrs. Franklin. Of course Patty hadn't seen the rats, and didn't know about the fainting spells. Those were Mrs. Puhn's little secrets, and as long as they stayed secret, Mrs. Puhn could stay on Sparroway Street.

Mrs. Puhn began the long and difficult task of getting back on her feet. She began by rolling onto her stomach and moving her hands and knees toward each other in a crawl. When she was finally on all fours, she reached for the kitchen table and pulled herself up.

Mrs. Puhn began cleaning. Patty mustn't see a mess on the floor. And she mustn't see one of the rats — not a one.

"She'd have me in a home by the end of the week," whispered Mrs. Puhn.

Admittedly, this is a lot of time to spend on characterization for a short story of 5,000 words, but the success of the entire story — not to mention the terror it causes in the reader — hinges completely on the proper characterization of Mrs. Puhn. Later in the story, when she is in peril, the reader feels for her, cares about her, and is truly afraid that something bad might happen to her.

Stereotypical characters

Sometimes in short fiction you can get away with less than full characterization. Here's where common stereotypes can be of use. For example, if they are simply in the story to advance the plot, authority figures need not be described in great detail. You might have a policeman in your story who is described simply as "a young policeman in uniform" or "an undercover detective in a dark blue suit." Or how about the "neighborhood bully," "the nosy neighbor," or the "nice old lady down the street." Each of these few-word descriptions conjures up an image in the reader's mind, and that image is more than enough to move the story forward. Such minor characters often just provide information, and once they've said their piece they're gone. It doesn't make sense to waste valuable words on information the reader doesn't need to know. If you're going to spend time on characterization in short fiction, spend it on your main characters.

Sympathetic characters

Sympathetic characters — or more simply put, characters that we care about — are a mainstay of horror fiction. That's why you so often see novels that feature women and children in peril. It's easy to feel sorry or be afraid for a woman being pursued by an axe-wielding maniac or for a child haunted by demons in his very own bedroom.

What would William Peter Blatty's *The Exorcist* have been if instead of 11-year-old Reagan MacNeil (the Linda Blair character in the film version) being possessed by the devil, it had been a middle-aged man? And what would have become of Stephen King's novel *The Shining* if instead of Jack Torrance going insane and trying to kill his wife and young son, it was the wife who had been affected by the madness of the Overlook Hotel? Somehow, it just doesn't seem to work as well, and it never would have worked as well as it did if the character of Jack Torrance (made famous by Jack Nicholson in Stanley Kubrick's film version) had not been so meticulously created by King.

Unsympathetic characters

Sometimes, the main character of your story must be absolutely reprehensible, a bad person who cheats and abuses those around him — even those who try to respond to his actions with kindness.

These characters usually get what's coming to them in the end, and the reader usually cheers when it happens. These types of stories are called Just Deserts stories and have been a mainstay of the horror genre since there were horror stories to tell. If you're not sure what's meant by a Just Deserts story, take a look at the pages of a *Tales from the Crypt* comic or watch an episode or two of the television show of the same name.

The success of these stories requires that the reader dislike the main character, but there must still be something about the character with which the reader can identify. If the character's fault is, say, greed, the reader must be able to recognize a little of his or her own greed within the character. In this way Just Deserts stories also become moral tales because at the end of the story the reader is able to think, "There but for the grace of God go I."

One of the most fun Just Deserts stories I've written was "Sex Starved," which appeared in the erotic horror anthology *Hot Blood: Deadly after Dark*. In the story, an overweight man marries a beautiful Mexican woman, who has wed him just to live in the United States. When he wants sex, she says she won't do anything with him until he loses 150 pounds. He starves himself and loses the weight, and when they finally have sex he's so hungry he eats her — literally. A Just Deserts story, if there ever was one.

How many characters do you need?

One question I'm often asked by my students is how many characters a short story or novel should have. It seems an odd question at first, and it often brings to mind the film *Amadeus* and the answer Mozart gives when the Emperor tells him that his new opera is near perfect, but there are just too many notes. Mozart replies, "I assure you, Emperor, I used only the number of notes I required. No more and no less."

Of course you should use only the number of characters you need to tell the story, but keep in mind that once you have three or four characters in a short story, keeping track of them all throughout the story could tax the reader's attention. You might want to consider combining characters to cut down on the number in your story. For example, if you have a policeman and a newspaper editor who both provide information that moves the plot forward, why not eliminate one of the characters and give the other a second appearance?

Another tip regarding characters is to make sure that all their names sound different, and that each name helps the reader get a feel for the character. This might sound obvious or silly, but having characters whose names begin even with the same letter can be a source of confusion. If your hero's name is Larry, don't name his wife or girlfriend Lilith or Laura. And if the female lead is a menace, don't name her Daisy unless you want to work a sense of irony into the story.

As for novels, the number of characters you can use is limited only by your imagination and your ability to keep multiple characters clear in your own mind and in the mind of the reader. As long as the characters are well drawn and serve a purpose, a novel can have a cast of thousands — and some generational sagas in the historical and romance genres do.

A Few Words With...

Gary A. Braunbeck

on writing horror short stories

EDO VAN BELKOM: You've been writing and selling short horror fiction at a terrific rate the past few years. How did you get from where you started to where you are now?

GARY A. BRAUNBECK: Public transportation is how I get most places. Seriously, though, I have always made it a point to read not only within the genre, but outside it as much as possible. I realized early on that you can't create anything worthwhile in a vacuum. I also made it a rule early on not to try to copy people like King, Straub, Poe, Lovecraft, and Shirley Jackson. I "got" to where I am now by promising myself always to practice my craft so that I am a better writer today than I was yesterday. I think there's no better way to do that — and measure your growth as a craftsman — than by writing short stories.

EDO VAN BELKOM: What do you find most difficult about writing a good horror story? Most easy?

GARY A. BRAUNBECK: The most difficult thing for me is not to think of a piece in terms of a "horror"; you set yourself up for failure if you begin by thinking, "I'm going to write a horror story." Whether you know it or not, you unconsciously accept too many boundaries by doing that — "It's horror, so this element has to be present, and this element, and then of course you have to have something like this happen...." It's too limiting if you think in terms of "horror" rather than "story." My stories just turn out to be somewhat horrific, and that's fine by me. The easiest thing for me has always been characterization and dialogue. A writer should know his/her own strengths and not be afraid to say so; I think I write solid characters and damn good dialogue.

EDO VAN BELKOM: How important are persistence and discipline to someone like you?

GARY A. BRAUNBECK: They're essential, but I think that's a given. I try not to be discouraged when pieces are rejected, and I write a minimum of 2,500 words a day. You cannot be a successful writer without performing that holy chore every single day — and don't worry if what you write on any given day turns out to be twaddle — you'll do better tomorrow, or later this afternoon, or, hey, maybe if I stay up real late tonight I can fix it....

Gary A. Braunbeck is the author of more than 130 published short stories, as well as the acclaimed collection Things Left Behind *and the novel* The Indifference of Heaven.

Plotting

The seven-step story

Storytelling is an art form, whether it be in horror or any other genre. After 150 short story sales in the ten years since I sold my first story, I've learned how stories work and how they don't work, and I've been able to use that knowledge to write stories in not only the horror genre but also in the genres of science fiction, mystery, and erotica, as well as in the mainstream. Learning how to tell a good story is the hard part, while learning the rules of a particular genre is as easy as reading works within it. (I was once told by a television producer that he would love to use new writers, but it was too difficult to teach them the format of writing for television. This infuriated me, because the presumption was that learning how to format a teleplay was more difficult — and more important — than knowing how to tell a compelling story.)

Luckily the ground rules of good storytelling aren't that hard to learn. Good stories need certain elements to work properly, just as a automobile needs to have an engine, transmission, axle, etc., to roll on down the highway. Many books might give tips on plotting, but I've never come across an explanation as simple to understand and as easily adapted as the one outlined by science fiction writer and editor Algis Budrys in Part One of his "Writing" column in the January 1993, Issue Number 1, of *Tomorrow* magazine. It's reproduced here as Table 1.

Over the years in teaching various writing classes, I've made some changes to it, even used it once or twice myself to create a story around an idea I had. So while the explanation of the principles is wholly my own, they had their genesis with the Budrys' article.

Now, let's get down to business.

TABLE 1

the seven-step story

1. BEGINNING	2. MIDDLE	3. END
(1) Character	(4) An attempt to solve the problem	(7) Validation
(2) In a context	(5) Unexpected failure (Problem is more difficult than first perceived)	
(3) With a problem	(6) Success or failure	

Every story has a beginning, a middle, and an end. One could argue that some stories lack endings, or lack a beginning, or are devoid of all three. (My personal pet peeve is with literary stories that have no discernible plotline at all. I call these stories "plot optional.") True, many short-short stories and vignettes — slice-of-life stories that are more a single scene than a complete story — do not have all three elements, but the type of stories to which this three-part model applies are the ones you'll be likely to read in a horror magazine or anthology. Every once in a while an arty literary story makes it into a horror publication, but for the most part, popular horror stories have beginnings, middles, and ends.

Let's start at the beginning, plotting a horror story as we go along.

1. The beginning

The beginning is obviously a very important part of your story. If it's doing its job, it will grab the reader's attention and make him or her want to read on.

(1) A character

Stories are about characters, and your main character (with one exception) should be likable or sympathetic, so that when he or she gets into peril, the reader will care whether or not your character makes it out alive. The one exception, as mentioned earlier, is the main character in a Just Deserts story. That character can be as disgusting as you can realistically make him because you want the reader to harumph, "Good!" when he gets it in the end.

In our story, the character will be Melissa, 24 years old, and a new college graduate who has just inherited a house and piece of property from a recently deceased aunt. Not knowing what she wants to do with her life, she considers converting the place into a bed and breakfast. Remember that our main character should be sympathetic, so we've already made great strides toward that by making her a) a woman, b) young, c) intelligent (a recent college grad), and d) self-reliant and self-confident — she wants to start her own business and make something of her life.

(2) In a context

Now that we have a character, we need a time and a place for the character to have her little adventure. The right setting for this type of story would be where cool winds blow, where there are shadows in the forest, and where there are colorful local characters that will be a good foil for Melissa's big-city upbringing. And since there should be a reasonable expectation that her bed and breakfast idea will work, the setting has to be a touristy area. That leaves us with plenty of choices, but something about New England seems to be a good fit. Let's say this property is in Vermont (which suggests the possibility of winter business during ski season), outside a town called Murphy's Corner. (This detail leaves us open to a curse or local ghost involving Murphy... if we need it.) Now that we have a place, we need to give our context a time. Since there's really nothing that can be gained by setting the story in an earlier time — and that, in fact, would make the old house newer — we'll just set it in the present day.

(3)   With a problem

Say we began the story with Melissa getting off the train at Murphy's Corner, with a map and deed to the property in her hand. She was hoping there would be a cab at the station to take her to her new place, but there's no one there, and no one else got off the train besides her. According to the map, the property doesn't look to be too far from the station. She decides to walk. That's just the action occurring at the start. While this is happening, the information about her character and her dreams for the place can be sprinkled about. This takes us from the station to the property, and by the time we get to the house, we have an idea that Melissa is a bit of a dreamer and her thoughts about fixing the place up and running it as a bed and breakfast are probably a little too hopeful.

When the property comes into view, it is so run down that she doesn't believe she's got the right address. (We could even set this up further by having her pass very well-maintained, even fancy homes all along the road leading up to her place.) She checks the address, even asks a passing motorist if she's got the right number. The motorist, a toothless, local blue-collar type (remember the colorful local characters; also, here's where a stereotypical character comes into play), asks her if she's the one who now owns the place, and when she says, "Yes," he laughs and tells her, "Good luck! You're going to need it!"

And so we come to Melissa's problem. The house on the property is so neglected, it would take an army of cleaners and builders a year to get it into shape. She feels sorry for herself, but only for a moment, then she marches up to the house, goes inside, and before the sun goes down, begins cleaning a spot where she can sleep.

We have now finished the beginning of our story. We have a character (Melissa), in a context (she has inherited a piece of property in present-day Vermont that she wants to convert into a bed and breakfast), with a problem (the place is so badly run down that it would make more sense for her to level the house and build something brand new on the site).

Character. Context. Problem.

That's the end of the beginning.

2. The middle

The middle is the heart of all stories. It's where all the good stuff takes place, and in a horror story, it's where you'll find most of the frights.

(4) An attempt to solve the problem

We've created Melissa, our main character, a strong-willed, self-assured young woman. When she's confronted by the condition of the house, she might complain for a while, but sooner or later she will get down to work. It is very important that she make the attempt to solve the problem herself and not wait around for someone else to solve it for her. For example, if she were a rich woman, she could call somebody in to do the work for her, or she could check into a hotel and wait for her boyfriend and his friends to arrive to fix the place up. Both are logical, perhaps even practical, but neither of them puts our character in the middle of the story. When we see Melissa down on her knees, scrubbing the floor and hammering nails and sweeping dust we root for her, hoping she succeeds.

But what if Melissa got down to work, worked really hard, got the place looking half-decent, then opened the bed and breakfast, and went on to run a successful business? It's a perfectly reasonable sequence of events that would likely happen in most such situations. However, if she succeeded on her first try, the story would be quite boring. Who wants to read stories about people succeeding first time out? Fact is, the first attempt your character makes to solve the problem must end in failure, and the problem must get worse.

(5) Unexpected failure (Problem is more difficult than first perceived)

Melissa makes it through the first night without much difficulty, although the wind was creaking through the house and she felt a chill passing through her all night long. These details provide a little bit of foreshadowing and set up events that will come later in the story.

Now with the morning sun bright in the sky, plenty of light to work with, and a determination to get things done right, Melissa is feeling good. Things are bad, but not so bad. However, she soon realizes that things are a lot worse than they seem. This realization could be shown in one of two ways. The problems with the house could mount — such as rotten floorboards giving way, or vermin in the walls, or perhaps a locked room for which the lawyer neglected to give her a key — or the house could turn out to be not so bad, nothing a good cleaning wouldn't fix, and then on her second night she could begin to hear voices, suffer great anxiety while she sleeps, or sleep soundly through the night, but wake up on the back porch with no recollection of how she got there.

This is where all the real action takes place. Every time she tries to make something better, it only gets worse. When she tries to find out about the supernatural entity in the house, she discovers that it is reputed to have been the cause of many violent deaths over the years. These are only a few suggestions. The plot can take as many twists and turns and develop as many complications as you like. However, if you're writing a short story, include three to five extra problems after the initial one, and that will give you enough material for about 5,000 words. Each problem should build on the one before until things come to a head as the story climaxes with one, all-or-nothing final attempt to solve the situation.

(6) Success or failure

This is an obvious next step. I have called it "Success or failure," but Algis Budrys used the phrase "Victory or death" in his article, which in some ways might be more correct, although it is entirely possible (although not as dramatic) for our heroine to fail but not die in the process.

In our story, this step would likely take this form: Things between Melissa and the demon haunting her house come to a head. She makes preparations (either making plans herself or perhaps calling in the help of some self-styled ghostbusters) for a final, winner-take-all confrontation. She will defeat the monster or die trying.

Stories in which the hero or heroine succeed are common enough (most ghost and monster stories end that way; e.g., Peter Benchley's *Jaws*), but there are many memorable tales in which the heroes or heroines fail despite their best efforts. A few excellent examples of this type of ending include Ira Levin's *Rosemary's Baby,* in which Rosemary gives birth to Satan's child and loves it as any mother would love her child; Stephen King's *Carrie,* in which Carrie loses out in the struggle to be just like all the other teenagers and destroys them all in the end; and Thomas Harris's *Silence of the Lambs,* in which Hannibal Lector gets away in the end, leaving the door open for the sequel, *Hannibal.*

Ending a horror story with the triumph of evil over good may leave open the possibility of a sequel, but that's not the only reason to end a story this way, nor is it the best one. Giving the reader the sense that the horror is not over, even in those stories in which the monster is defeated, is one of the tenets of the horror genre: No matter how hard you try, you will never be able to defeat evil completely. It will wait in the background (much like Lovecraft's Cthulhu monsters) until it sees its opportunity to return.

3. *The end*

The end of the story wraps things up, sometimes very neatly, sometimes not. In horror, the end can also be where the biggest and best frights occur, the ones that stay with you for a long, long time.

(7) Validation

Budrys explains validation as simply some character stepping forward to say something like, "Who was that masked man? I wanted to thank him," so that the reader knows that the story is now over. Validation gives the reader this assurance, and as a result, provides closure.

But validation can be more than that. If done correctly, it can provide a summation of the story's overall theme or set up another story yet to come (the evil has been defeated... for now). In horror, it can also give the story a neat surprise, supplying not only closure but a shock at the point at which readers will remember it most.

Included here is the end to my short story, "Family Ties." A young newspaper reporter hears screams coming from the railway lines near his house. After some research, he learns that a young woman died on the tracks some years ago. She was pregnant at the time of her death, and it turns out that her ghost is calling him because it needs a father for her child. He goes to investigate the tracks and is trapped, held there by the ghost as a train passes over the tracks.

And now the ending:

Susan sat in the rocking chair in the living room, knitting. The chair had been a gift from Gardner's parents. It was old and worn and a bit uncomfortable, but Susan loved it. What she looked forward to most of all was rocking in it while her child suckled at her breast. A simple pleasure, like knitting booties and sweaters and mittens.

But then, everything had been wonderful so far, not the least of which had been Gardner's attitude. He'd turned out to be more enthusiastic about the baby than she could have ever imagined. He was a good man. Helpful and supportive. She knew, intuitively, that he'd be a good father to her child. It was one less thing to worry about, and it had made the uncertainty about how their lives would change in four short months so much easier to handle.

She glanced at the clock.

It was getting late, but Susan wasn't concerned. She'd been married to a newspaper man far too long to start worrying whenever he didn't call or came home late.

She reached down for another ball of yarn when she heard something.

The scream.

She gave a little laugh.

I've finally heard it, she thought.

I can't wait to tell Gardner when he gets home.

The seven-step novel

Using the Seven Steps is a great way to plot out a short story, but it is just as effective as a means of plotting an entire novel. The only difference is that the novel will include a main plot with far more complications in the middle, and — most important — several other seven-step plotlines interwoven with each other or occuring alongside each other, until they all achieve step six, Success or Failure, together.

So if you wanted to turn our story about Melissa into a novel, you would give her a boyfriend who doesn't want her to move away. He might call her, then finally come to get her and take her away, only to be killed by the evil haunting her newly acquired home. Then you might include a storyline about the town mayor who had plans of buying the property with the hope of leveling the house and building new homes for his two children or a new hotel for the town. Throw in a good-intentioned neighbor with whom Melissa gets along well (who might die horribly along the way), and finally a town sheriff who's single and who's attracted to Melissa. The sheriff could also know the secret of the house and he might be the one to help her fight the evil in the end. It's basically the same story, but with more characters (remember, you're allowed that in a novel) and several more plotlines, all of which gives the novelist far more room to move and much more material to twist and turn along the way.

Themes: More Than Just a Scary Story

Theme is the primary statement, suggestion, or implication of a literary work. It describes that portion of the work that comments on the human condition.

Sounds simple enough, but what exactly does it mean?

Science fiction author Robert J. Sawyer explains theme in this way: If you can say what a story is about without referring to the plot (the events of the story), then you've found its theme.

This explanation works very well with Mary Wollstonecraft Shelley's *Frankenstein*. If we ask what the book is about, but do not refer in our answer to the plot of the monster's creation and persecution by the villagers, the answer might be that it is about the terrible consequences to be paid when men of science try to play the role of God, the role of creator.

If the same question were to be asked about Joseph Conrad's *Heart of Darkness* (the basis for the film *Apocalypse Now,* among others) the answer would be that it is about the utterly thin line between civilization and savagery and how easily that line can be crossed.

Of course, not all stories and novels have themes, and not all authors start writing with a theme in mind. Quite often, a theme is incorporated into a novel unconsciously during its creation (suggested by its subject matter or storyline) and is only discovered after the piece is finished — sometimes not even by the author. The theme of a piece of fiction is a nebulous entity, open to debate, discussion, and interpretation. It is something that a new writer should be aware of but not obsessed with. After all, there are plenty of other aspects of writing horror fiction to be mastered before you need worry about including a theme in your story or novel.

6
how does horror work?

Horror fiction relies on a number of techniques for effectiveness. This chapter examines just a few of these.

Suspension of Disbelief

Because horror is a subgenre of speculative fiction, it works on the premise of "What if?" In the opening chapter of this book I used the example, "What if the dead rose up from their graves with an insatiable hunger for human flesh?" For one thing, there would be chaos. And if the story wasn't set up right, there would also be howls of laughter from the reader.

Incredible things can happen in horror fiction, but the reader has to be able to believe that these same incredible things can happen in real life. This believability is called suspension of disbelief: the groundwork laid down by the author allows you, as a reader, to be absolutely willing to believe that the dead can rise up from their graves.

Fine, but how does an author achieve that?

In fairy tales, the standard opening line is "Once upon a time." While that sounds like a fairly soft and poetic phrase, it is actually a device to aid a reader's suspension of disbelief. It tells the reader that these events happened once upon a time; not last week, not last year, but at some point in the past. That frees up the imagination of the reader to place the story in any time he or she chooses, any time that seems right.

The film *Star Wars* begins with the now famous line "A long time ago, in a galaxy far, far away," and so suspends a movie-goer's disbelief. We perceive science fiction and futuristic-looking movies to take place in the future — our future. This one line turns that notion on its head, putting the story somewhere else and in the past.

In horror fiction, especially horror fiction with a supernatural element, suspension of disbelief is achieved through the details that make an incredible occurrence believable. For example, would William Peter Blatty's portrayal of an exorcism have been believable if he hadn't been well versed in the doctrine and rites of the Catholic church? If you, as an author, show the reader that you know what you're talking about, the line between what is real and what is a plausible fabrication blurs until the two are indistinguishable. In many ways, what you shoot for is verisimilitude, which is a fancy word for something that *sounds true*. If the fantastic element you're writing about sounds as if it *could* be true, you've suspended the reader's disbelief.

But as well as details work, it's sometimes difficult to know which ones will satisfy the reader and which ones won't. It all comes down to what feels right. In the vampire story "Lip-O-Suction," I wrote about a doctor vampire who drinks human fat rather than human blood — a lipophilic vampire. One of his patients becomes a vampire as well during the course of his treatment. I originally had the fat-sucking vampire be surprised to have created another of his kind because the chances of the condition being transferred to another were astronomically low, but none of the members of my writers' group at the time believed that. It was a roadblock to the story. If the vampire had thought he might spread his condition, then he shouldn't have risked it, and if it were even remotely possible, then why was he so surprised by it when it happened? And so I changed the story, and had the vampire say —

"It is a rare disease among vampires and, despite what has happened to you, was for centuries believed to be noncommunicable.

That is why I felt secure in opening this business. I feed easily and well, and I help people, make them happy. It is a good life."

This worked well, was plausible, and I sold the story, eventually reprinting it in my collection *Death Drives a Semi*.

Another way to suspend a reader's disbelief is through setting. This is especially effective in horror and fantasy fiction in which incredible events need an incredible location.

For example, would Jack Torrance's madness have been as effective, or the novel as scary as it was, if Stephen King has set *The Shining* anywhere other than the truly eerie Overlook Hotel? Would the events in Ray Bradbury's *Something Wicked This Way Comes* have been believable if he hadn't taken the time to paint a vivid portrait, first of the small community of Green Town, Illinois, and then to show us that this October was quite different from those in the past? Once that groundwork has been laid, anything can — and does — happen.

To suspend a reader's disbelief, an author might also treat the extraordinary as if it were absolutely ordinary. One of the first modern novels to insert the supernatural into the present day was *The Night Stalker* by Jeff Rice. Rice placed a vampire in present-day Las Vegas and put newspaper reporter Carl Kolchak on the vampire's trail. The novel is written in a straightforward manner with little or no attempt to explain how or why the vampire is there: it just is. The reader is forced to accept this fact because the book does not allow for any other reaction. If the reader doesn't believe, then the reader is part of the conspiracy trying to dismiss Kolchak as a crazy, washed-up reporter. The novel was the basis for the most successful made-for-television movie of its time and also spawned a television series by the same name, starring Darren McGavin.

The Threat Is Real

Horror works best when it is possible for characters to be confronted by the forces of evil at any time, in any place, preferably without warning. Similarly, those forces should be as scary as you can make them. If your monster isn't all that terrifying, or the damage it inflicts isn't all that severe, the reader isn't going to be frightened by your character's predicament. Take the shark in Peter Benchley's *Jaws*. It is able to strike any time and any place; it is cunning, merciless, and unstoppable; and when it strikes, it kills without prejudice. The ultimate killing machine, an ultimate evil.

On a slightly different note, one might think that the most valuable thing that can be taken away from one is one's life. That's a good starting point, and most horror heroes and heroines are dealing with monsters and demons that will ultimately take their lives or die trying. Loss of life is one of the biggest threats a character can experience, but not the biggest. As I've mentioned in an earlier chapter, I've always thought that a threat to someone else, most often a loved one (son, daughter, spouse), is the most powerful threat of all. Even in *The Exorcist* we are told that the possessed is never the target of the demon; rather the real target is those around the afflicted one.

So, you see, even the devil knows what constitutes the biggest threat to the human psyche.

Sympathetic Characters in Peril

As already mentioned in chapter 5, to capture and keep a reader's attention, horror stories need sympathetic characters.

Would we care if an 87-year-old man just diagnosed with cancer sets out to confront the demon haunting the mansion on the hill? Probably not. You'd say he had a long and (we hope) rich life, and that anyway it was his time to go. Similarly, would you be saddened by the horrific death of a serial rapist who has just robbed a bank and killed the teller that served him? Nope. You'd cheer and say, "It's about bloody time!" However, would you fear for the young mother who's already lost her husband and brother to the demon and is now fighting off the terror while she holds her newborn baby in her arms? Of course you'd fear for her life, for the life of the baby, and you'd cheer her on. With every blow that she strikes to fell the demon, you're right alongside with her, striking the blows as well.

If you want your readers to go the distance and take the journey through your short story or novel, you have to make them care for your characters (with the exception of those villains who get what's coming to them in Just Deserts stories; see chapter 5, Unsympathetic characters, for more about those).

Enough said.

Point of View (POV)

One of the most important things to learn about the art of writing any kind of fiction — and one of the most difficult things for new writers to learn — is how to handle point of view, or POV.

Simply stated, POV is the agent (usually a character in the story or novel) through whose eyes a piece of fiction is presented. This character's thoughts are revealed directly to the reader. Point of view is generally limited to a single character in a short story; in a novel, several characters can provide the POV at different times during the course of the story. However, you should note that if you want to avoid confusing the reader, you should make sure each scene has only a single POV character. A novel that uses many different characters for POV — and as many as a dozen or more viewpoints can be used — is called a multiple-viewpoint novel.

Point of view changes according to character. For example, what if an old woman, a young man, a teenager, and a little girl had to describe a couple kissing on a park bench? How would their points of view differ?

Old woman

She noticed a couple in an amorous embrace on the park bench to her right. They were so young and seemed not to care who saw them. Well good for them. Life's too short to worry about who's looking anyway.

Young man

He noticed a couple necking on the park bench to his right. From what he could see she was rather pretty and seemed to be enjoying herself. As he walked by, doing his best not to stare, he wondered if Margaret was doing anything tonight.

Teenage boy

He was on his way to the skateboard park when he noticed a couple making out on the bench to his right. Man, she's really putting out, and out in public too. Cool!

Little girl

As she walked along the path she noticed a mommy and a daddy kissing on the bench near the swings. Mommy kissed daddy like

that when he brought her flowers on her birthday. I wonder how
old that mommy is today?

These examples are somewhat simplistic and perhaps overwritten to illustrate a point, but they do show that different characters have different ways of looking at the world around them. Even the words used to describe the couple's action change with each POV, from "an amorous embrace," seen through the eyes of the old woman, to simply "kissing" when see by the young girl. That is why before you begin writing a story or novel, you must give some thought to which of the characters would be the best one to tell the story.

If you're still uncertain what is meant by POV, pick up a novel, open it up to a scene and start reading. You'll soon become aware of the following:

(1) When you read passages about a character's inner feelings, you've found the POV character, the character through which the entire scene is being viewed.

(2) When you read passages of straight description, that's what you might call the narrator talking, since what is being described is not filtered through the POV character but simply reported by someone or something who describes only what can be seen. (Orson Scott Card in his excellent book *Characters and Viewpoint* describes the narrator as a camera fixed somewhere up in the corner of a scene reporting what's happening without comment or prejudice.)

(3) When you read about other characters, observe closely how their emotions are described, for that's how you'll learn the most about how to use POV to your advantage — and how to avoid its inevitable pitfalls.

To illustrate the above points, here's a scene from my short story "The Rug," in which an old woman, Edna Dowell, is the POV character. She's being shaken down by her landlord, Marty Genetti, for overdue rent money. The (1), (2), and (3) in the right-hand column correspond to the points listed above:

1. *He went into the kitchen, Edna following as fast as*   *(1)*
   her feet could take her.

2. *"What's with all the cookie tins? That where you keep*
   your stash?" He started taking the tins off the shelf and   *(2)*
   opening them one by one.

3. *Edna did keep some bills and a few coins in a couple of the tins, but that was emergency money for doctor's visits and medicine. If he took that she'd literally be without a penny to her name.*   *(1)*

4. *"Stop it!" she shouted. "Stop!"*   *(2)*

5. *"Oh, am I getting warm?" he laughed, almost as if he was enjoying his little act of terrorism.*   *(3)*

6. *"Please, stop!" she pleaded again, but her words only seemed to spur him on.*   *(3)*

7. *He found a Christie's tin with some money in it. "All right," he said. "This is a start.... Let's see what else we can find."*   *(2)*

8. *Edna began trembling in frustration and anger. If he kept on like this he was bound to find her pension check and then she'd be left with nothing. She had to do something, but what?*   *(1)*

9. *"Heh-hey! Here's a twenty," he said, looking more and more like a neighborhood bully shaking down kids for candies.*   *(3)*

10. *Edna glanced at the kitchen counter. Her rolling pin was there, a chipped and cracked rolling pin made out of marble she'd found years ago in a dumpster behind the Commisso Brothers Italian Bakery. She stared at the rolling pin for what seemed like forever, then finally picked it up...*   *(2)* *(1)*

11. *"You gotta have a piggy bank here somewhere."*   *(2)*

12. *...raised it over her head...*   *(2)*

13. *"Or maybe a roll of pennies — "*   *(2)*

14. *...and let it fall.*   *(2)*

(1) Paragraphs 1, 3, and 8 are from Edna Dowell's POV. They contain her thoughts and emotions, things we couldn't possibly know if she weren't the POV character, starting with the very first sentence, "...as fast as her feet could take her." If we weren't in her POV, how could we know that as slow as she's probably moving, it's as fast as her feet can move? Paragraph 10 begins with straight reportage (2) until we are told that Edna stared at the rolling pin. Although the word "seemed" is used (more on that coming up) since it is from her POV, it is a description of how time appeared to stand still for her as she looked at the rolling pin and thought about what she might be able to do with it.

(2) Paragraphs 2, 4, 7, the first part of paragraph 10, and paragraphs 11 to 14 are all told by the narrator (or relayed to the reader through the camera positioned high up in one corner of the room. They are straightforward reportage and have no subjective viewpoint.

(3) Paragraphs 5, 6, and 9 are the tricky ones. They convey emotions and thoughts assigned to the character of Marty Genetti. But these are only guesses as to what's really going on in his mind, because Marty isn't the POV character — Edna is.

In paragraph 5, his laugh is described: "almost as if he was enjoying his little act of terrorism." Obviously, he *is* enjoying it, but since we can't get into his head to know for sure what's going on in there we have to guess — hence the phrase, "almost as if." This lets us say what we want to without saying it with authority.

In paragraph 6, she pleads with him, but "her words only seemed to spur him on." Of course he was spurred on by her words, but once again, since we aren't in Marty's head, we can't actually say that for certain; we can only guess. Maybe he's enjoying the hunt, maybe he's enjoying playing the part of the bully, and maybe her pleading adds to his enjoyment. We have to make a guess, and so describe it by using the word "seemed" to allow for a slight measure of uncertainty.

In paragraph 9, Marty's appearance is described as "looking more and more like a neighborhood bully shaking down kids for candies." This simile is a way of describing what might be going on in Marty's mind. Maybe he's reliving the days when he and his teenage friends rolled oldtimers for beer money. Saying that he looks "like" or looks "as if" is another way of making a POV-type statement about a non-POV character. It also tells us a little about Edna's character, because the way Marty looks reminds her of something similar she's seen in the past.

Once you know what to look for in terms of POV, with a little practice you'll be able to recognize the techniques your favorite authors use to maintain a scene's POV. You might not want to use those techniques when you write your story or novel, but you should know how to use them if you must. Quite often in horror fiction a change of tense or viewpoint is used to indicate a shift from the narrator to the monster or evil entity's mind; its feel and rhythm must be different from that of the narrator.

Sample 4 gives an example of one scene told through two different points of view. But now that we've reviewed the basics of POV, there are some common POV variations to keep in mind.

First person

In a first-person narrative, the character telling the story refers to himself as the "I": "I walked down to the corner bar and ordered a drink. The bartender looked at me strangely, then smiled broadly until I could easily make out his two very long fangs." This POV can seem deceptively easy to write, but it is in fact very difficult to write well. The entire story must be filtered through the "I" character's mind, and that can sometimes be difficult to do consistently. The first-person POV can also be used along with the present tense, which would make the sentence above read, "I walk down to the corner bar and order a drink. The bartender looks at me strangely, then smiles broadly, and I can see that he's got two very long fangs." Many writers seem to use the first-person present-tense because they think it makes their work more literary. I think it just makes it more pretentious. Before a writer begins a piece he or she must decide what narrative viewpoint would suit the story best, and on very few occasions will that be first-person present-tense. I myself have used it only once in more than 150 short stories, and that was because the story in question, "But Somebody's Got to Do It," is told from the POV of a zombie who can know nothing other than what is happening at the moment. This is one of the pitfalls of first-person present-tense: it allows a character to describe the story only as it is happening. Sure, you can add other events through flashback or via other POV characters, but the moment you do so you call into question the use of the first-person present-tense viewpoint.

Second person

In a second-person narrative, the story is told with "you" as the POV character. Using this technique, our sample sentence reads like this: "You walked down to the corner bar and ordered a drink. The bartender

sample 4
one scene/two points of view

The following is the same scene (two cops responding to a call at a bank in which shots have been fired) told from two different points of view. The version on the left is from the point of view of an older, more experienced policeman. The version on the right is from the point of view of a rookie.

1
"Borden Street's the next one on the right," said officer Sparks. "At that convenience store."

"Yeah, I know where it is," answered Sergeant Maguire, turning the wheel hard right.

"That's the bank there!"

2
"Stay down and out of the way," said the sergeant. The kid had been with him for less than a week and sometimes wanted to do things in a rush.

"Right," nodded Sparks.

3
The two police officers took up positions behind the cruiser and waited for backup.

"See anything?" asked Maguire.

Sparks shook his head. "No."

"All right. We'll wait for back-up. Then we'll move in."

4
They waited for several seconds, then Sparks said, "I think I see something."

Maguire squinted and tried to look more deeply into the bank. "I don't see anything."

5
"Sure, there's two of them and they're slipping out the back. We got to do something."

"We'll wait, they might be armed — "

Too late. Sparks was already up and running toward the bank.

1
"Borden Street's the next one on the right," said officer Sparks. "At that convenience store."

"Yeah, I know where it is," answered Sergeant Maguire, turning the wheel hard right.

"That's the bank there!"

2
"Stay down and out of the way," said the sergeant.

"Right," nodded Sparks, just a little sarcastically.

3
The two police officers took up positions behind the cruiser and waited for backup.

"See anything?" asked Maguire.

Sparks shook his head. "No."

"All right. We'll wait for back-up. Then we'll move in."

4
Sparks trained his gun on the bank and with each passing second, he pictured the killer getting farther and farther away. If they waited any longer he'd be gone for good. They had to move now. "I think I see something," he said.

"I don't see anything."

5
"Sure, there's two of them and they're slipping out the back. We got to do something."

"We'll wait, they might be armed."

Stupid idiot, thought Maguire. What the hell does he think he's doing?

6   Sparks was halfway toward the bank when one of the front doors opened. A second later there was a man standing there with a mask on, holding a gun.

"He's got a gun!" shouted Maguire.

Sparks raised his weapon. "Put it down."

7   The masked man fired, three times.

Sparks fell to the ground.

Maguire emptied his revolver, and the masked man was thrown back against the side of the bank, then slowly slid down the wall.

And then, silence.

It's always wait for back-up with you, isn't it, thought Sparks. His partner might have had more experience, but he'd lost his edge. The last time he took a chance on something it was a cup of decaf.

6   Sparks got up and started running toward the bank. He was halfway there when one of the front doors opened.

"He's got a gun!"

Sparks saw the gun in the masked man's hand and said, "Put it down."

7   The masked man fired, three times.

Sparks felt the bullets hit his chest like punches from a heavy fist. The first one knocked the wind out of him. The second and third knocked him to the ground.

There were more gunshots then, and Sparks only hoped that Maguire hadn't waited too long before he fired.

Section 1: In both versions, this section is told by the narrator; no specific POV is being utilized. The events are simply reported as if viewed by an unbiased party (or camera) set up in the police car.

Section 2: In the version on the left, we get the first indication of who the point-of-view character is: the older cop, who has a comment to make about the kid always being in a hurry. In the version on the right, we learn that the young cop says, "Right," with a hint of sarcasm, which indicates that the version on the right is told from the younger cop's point of view. In the heat of the moment, it might not be apparent to the older cop that the word was meant sarcastically.

Section 3: Once again, this is straight reportage from the narrator.

Section 4: We see what sort of effect waiting has on each of the police officers. The older cop is much calmer than the younger one, who is eager to get into action — almost too eager, since he reports seeing something when we really didn't see anything from his POV.

Section 5: Here the differences between the two POVs become even greater, as the older cop insists they wait for back-up — and gives his opinion on the younger's actions — and the younger gives his opinion on the older being so by-the-book.

Section 6: This section is almost identical in both versions except that the way the action is described reflects the different vantage points of the two characters. Think of the scene as being filmed by two different cameras and you'll get a good idea of how the two POVs need to be written.

looked at you strangely, then smiled broadly until you could easily make out his two very long fangs." A change in tense from past to present would make it read, "You walk down to the corner bar and order a drink. The bartender looks at you strangely, then smiles broadly until you can see that he's got two very long fangs."

The second-person viewpoint is very rarely used, especially in the horror genre, but one of the best examples of a short story written in the second person, past tense is "Stab" by Lawrence Watt-Evans, published in the 1992 anthology *Metahorror,* edited by Dennis Etchison. And as seldom as the second person is used in short fiction, it is even more rarely used in novels. One exception — though not a horror novel — is Jay McIrney's *Bright Lights, Big City,* the basis for a film starring Michael J. Fox.

Third person

The third person is the most widely used of all the narrative points of view, and with good reason. It is the most flexible for writers, most readable to readers, and is so familiar to both as to seem invisible on the page. While first- and second-person points of view draw attention to themselves (first person: *look at me, I'm literary*; and second person: *look at me, I'm different*) and are hard to read, third person has become the natural way — an almost default format — of telling a story. In the third person, the sample sentences read, "Johnny Van Helsing walked down to the corner bar and ordered a drink. The bartender looked at him strangely, then smiled broadly until Van Helsing could easily make out his two very long fangs."

Use of the third person also makes it easier to incorporate flashbacks into your story — because they too are in the third person — and to use multiple viewpoints in a novel. Although the POV character changes, the narrative style does not, and this is less jarring to the reader than having one scene told by the "I" or the "you" and then another told by a totally different character with an actual name.

The present tense is least obtrusive when used with the third person, but all I've said before about present tense still applies here. In the third person present tense, our sample sentences would read, "Johnny Van Helsing walks down to the corner bar and orders a drink. The bartender looks at him strangely, then smiles broadly until Van Helsing sees that he's got two very long fangs."

If you're unsure which POV you should be using, try writing your story or a sample chapter using each of the different POVs to help you decide which one you like best or which one is the best fit with the kind of story you are writing.

Omniscient/Limited omniscient/Objective

The final POV variations are the omniscient and limited omniscient points of view. It sounds difficult, especially when you might still be trying to get a handle on first person and present tense, but it's really not all that hard.

Omniscient

Omniscient refers to the narrator's abilities. It means "all knowing," just as omnipotent means "all powerful." Up until now, I've explained the narrator as the objective observer who reports what is seen without commenting on it. The omniscient narrator knows exactly what is going on in every character's mind. In a story with an omniscient narrator, there is no POV character, because every character's thoughts are made known to the reader.

Although use of the omniscient narrator is a valid technique, it's probably the poorest one in the writer's arsenal. Part of the appeal of fiction is that it allows us to get deep within a character's mind, to know his or her thoughts and to discover the twisted way in which he or she looks upon the world. None of this is possible with an omniscient narrator. True, the reader gets to see inside all the characters' thoughts, but the probe isn't very deep into any of them, and the reading experience can be somewhat flat. In horror fiction, the omniscient narrator is an especially weak device because, on one hand, there can be no withheld information and, thus, little suspense, since we know what everyone is thinking. On the other hand, if the omniscient narrator has to withhold any information or any character's thoughts, the story is unsuccessful and a cheat.

Limited omniscient

The limited-omniscient POV is the one most commonly used by writers and is most familiar to readers. Simply put, in a story or novel told from a limited-omniscient POV, the narrator can reveal everything that goes on in the head of the POV character, but can only guess at what is happening in the minds of the others. This technique allows the writer to explore a character's thoughts and motivations and to paint the best portrait for the reader.

Objective

The objective POV is the opposite of the omniscient. While an omniscient narrator knows everything that's going on inside every character's head, the objective narrator knows nothing. The objective narrator is the camera that records what is happening, and never comments or judges any of it. Remember this one by thinking of the narrator as a reporter or police investigator who must be interested only in the facts and not in conjecture.

Showing versus Telling

Next to mastering the use of point of view, the most difficult thing about the craft of writing for new writers to grasp is the difference between showing and telling. Telling, which most aspiring writers are guilty of, is the stuff of poor writing and leaves fiction flat and lifeless. Showing, which most professional writers do with ease, is the mark of good fiction, making stories ring true with a crispness that engages the reader and makes reading a joy.

In the previous paragraph, I've just shown you the difference between showing and telling. If I had simply told you the difference it would have read something like, *Showing, good. Telling, bad.* Not very engaging, not very descriptive, and downright boring.

But how does showing and telling work in fiction? Let's say we wanted to create a female character who has a lot of money. How might we go about it? Here's how, both in telling and showing modes:

> **Telling:** *She was a wealthy woman, drove a fancy car, and spent a lot of money wherever she went.*

> **Showing:** *You could tell she had cash and she liked to spend it. She never left the house dressed in anything but Versace, carrying her credit cards in the smallest Chanel bag they made. She drove a Jaguar that looked as if it had just came out of the showroom, but you just knew she'd never wiped a smudge off its fender herself. And she always tipped the valet with a twenty, coming and going. What did it matter — her lawyer had soaked her ex-husband dry, and even if he hadn't, she was hardly the type to spend her own money anywhere when there were so many men out there eager to have her spend their money for them.*

The telling example gives us only a little simple information. The showing example, however, gives us both that simple bit of information along with a vivid portrait of the woman, who is shown to be not only rich and free with money, but also a beautiful woman who knows how to use her beauty to her advantage — a *femme fatale*.

Now, how about describing a scary monster who is terrorizing a camp site somewhere in Northern Ontario?

> **Telling:** *It was a huge monster with big teeth, sharp claws, and a nasty disposition.*

> **Showing:** *Even in a partial crouch it towered over the Winnebago. Something wet and slimy dripped from several of its razor-sharp teeth, while the others were all stained with blood. It had been startled by the first blast from the Buick's horn, but now that it had an idea where the sound was coming from, it looked ready to strip the land yacht down to its chassis.*

Showing versus telling. Get the idea now?

Not, "He was scared," but, "His pulse was racing and he had to fight to catch his breath. His knees were shaking too, but at least that told him he was alive."

Not, "The beast broke down the door," but, "A fisted hand blasted through the door like a sledgehammer, sending wood splinters flying in every direction." Not, "She stabbed him," but, "She pushed the tip of the blade down until it pierced his flesh, then she put her weight behind the hilt and pushed it all the way inside, scraping bone and sinew every inch of the way."

Try it yourself. Take a few everyday telling sentences like, "He looked mean," "She stood in the doorway, afraid," "The dog could turn wild at any moment," "This monster was different," and "He knew a lot about knives," and see what you can do to make them into showing sentences that paint a more vivid picture of the information that's being conveyed.

Exposition

Exposition is factual writing that provides background information necessary to the reader's understanding of a story, and without which a story will not work. It provides this information directly, as opposed to through thoughts or dialogue.

Exposition is also something to be wary of. Too much, and your story will seem to stop dead in its tracks. Too little, and your readers won't have the information they need to make the story a success.

In my own stories, passages of exposition almost always occur in the first five pages so that I can get the information out of the way and won't have to stop the story later on — when the piece is really rolling along — to explain something to the reader. I also don't want to just plant some information into the story that the reader will have to know five lines later — that's too much of a coincidence.

My best effort in terms of large amounts of information slipped invisibly into the narrative is probably "Ice Bridge," in which the whole process of carrying logs in trucks over frozen lakes during the winter in the interior of British Columbia had to be explained before the reader could start to enjoy the story. I can't relate all of it here, but here are the first few paragraphs of the story to give you an idea how information can be conveyed:

Here's a general rule that will help you remember that much more information can be conveyed through dialogue than through pure description:

three lines of dialogue = three pages of exposition

The continuous diesel-driven thrum of the loader was only occasionally drowned out by the crash of logs being dumped into place. The loud noise was followed by the faint groan of metal and the slight rumbling of frozen earth as the truck dutifully bowed to accept its load.

Rick Hartwick mixed his coffee with a plastic stir-stick and walked casually toward the far end of the office trailer. At the window, he blew across the top of his steaming cup and watched his breath freeze against the pane. Then he took a sip, wiped away the patch of ice that had formed on the glass, and watched his truck being loaded one last time.

As always, the loader, a Quebecois named Pierre Langlois, was making sure Rick's rig was piled heavy with spruce and pine logs, some of them more than three feet in diameter. Langlois liked Rick, and with good reason. Every other week throughout the season, Rick had provided Langlois with a bottle of Canadian Club. He'd been doing it for years now, ever since he'd called a loader an asshole during a card game and wound up driving trucks loaded with soft wood and air the rest of the winter.

He'd been lucky to hang on to his rig.

The next winter he began greasing Langlois' gears with the best 80 proof he could find and since then he'd never had a load under 30 tonnes and only a handful under 35.

He owned his rig now, as well a house in Prince George.

When I used to participate in a weekly writer's group, we'd call long passages of exposition, "Horking Chunks of Exposition." It was an apt description, mostly because it gave a derogatory connotation to exposition and kept me on my toes whenever I began writing purely informational prose. Later, as I read other writers more closely (and writers are always analyzing while they read), I realized that Stephen King rarely used more than two purely expositional paragraphs in a row without breaking them up with a line of action or dialogue. It's a handy rule to go by and will prevent your fiction from slowing to a snail's pace.

But of course, there are always exceptions to the rule. I once had to include in a story a long explanation of how homeless men were being rehabilitated in San Francisco. It could not be summarized or cut down, and it had to be explained fully before the story could continue. Rather than wrestle with trying to fit it seamlessly into the story, I simply stopped the story cold to explain it. So, in "A Wolf in Shepherd's Clothing," published in the anthology *When Will You Rage,* I wrote —

> *But unlike the other shelters along Jones and Eddy Streets, Father Oldman and the people of the Scott Mission didn't just give the city's discards a hot meal and a place to sleep, they actually worked to rehabilitate them.*
>
> *To give them a totally new way of life.*
>
> *It worked like this:*
>
> *After a homeless man has been taken in by the shelter, he is given new clothes, regular meals, and put on a program to rid him of any substance dependencies he might have. When he's deemed a suitable candidate and fit to travel he is moved to The Scott Ranch situated just north of the Muir Woods, where he is educated about the wonder of Gaia and how important it is that she be preserved in all her glory...*

The explanation went on for about a page and a half and I was able to resume the story afterward, but that was the only time I've ever done such a "wrong" thing. It's okay to do something wrong every once in a while, but keep in mind that you have to know the rules before you can know how and when to break them.

Scenes

Scenes are dramatic representations of what happens in a story and they should be used as often as possible, since a story or novel is, in reality, a collection of scenes linked by a single narrative.

In my first novel, *Wyrm Wolf,* I needed to flesh out the character of Father Wendel Oldman. Father Oldman is a priest running a shelter for the homeless in San Francisco, so he's obviously a good man, but he also happens to be a werewolf. I wanted to show that he was a good man, but one who could be absolutely brutal when he had to be. Rather than simply stating that as I've just done, I chose instead to show it by writing a scene in which these qualities would be obvious. I had him out looking for the renegade werewolf who had been killing off the homeless people in his care. During his search, he comes across an alley in which two men are raping a young woman. He stops the crime and administers his own type of justice, giving the men wounds that will help them remember their abhorrent behavior for the rest of their lives.

This scene showed that Father Oldman could be gentle, as he is with the woman, and fearsome, as he is with the men. That sort of character development wouldn't have been possible with even a dozen pages of exposition. Likewise, if you want to show a character's softer side, write a scene in which he or she is being thoughtful or kind, or in which he or she sheds a tear.

Dialogue

Dialogue must sound real. If your characters talk in language that is stilted or strained, your dialogue will draw attention to itself and the story could very well fall flat.

The next time you go out, listen to the way people talk. If you hear an interesting pronouncement or phrasing, repeat it over and over in your mind so that the next time you have to write a colorful character, his or her manner of speech will be there for you. And pay attention to how people of different ethnic backgrounds speak English. There's no easier way to make a supporting character stand out than to give him an ethnicity that will automatically make his name, speech, dress, and gestures different from those of the other characters in your story.

Try not to write ethnic speech too phonetically. If you have a character from the deep south or from someplace like Ireland, pick and choose the words you want to spell phonetically. When people with heavy accents actually speak, every word might very well be hacked and spliced, but in writing it's best to denote an accent with just a few well-placed apostrophes. Instead of your gun-toting sheriff telling the zombie terrorizing the town, "You're gonna wish ta hell you t'aint never been reborn, you stinkin', stumblin' rot-yellow-bellied bastid!" — which might be close to the way such a tirade would sound — you'd be better off writing it as, "You're gonna wish to hell you were never reborn, you stinkin', stumblin' rot-yellow-bellied bastard!" Small changes, I know. But though it doesn't take much on the page to conjure up an accent in a reader's mind, it's easy to cause a reader to stumble over awkward spellings. Best to make sure the words are clear before trying to add a dab of color.

I think writers are possessed of constantly functioning dopplegangers. No matter what happens in their personal lives — and I mean no matter what — their creative doppleganger stands aside and observes, comments, takes down ideas and schemes from a distance. It is, at once, a terrible and wonderful gift.

— RICHARD MATHESON

One final reminder about dialogue is that it should be appropriate for the age of your characters. A mother of 40 and a child over 5 will look at the world differently and will use different words to describe the same thing. For example, what an adult might call "the beast," the child might call "the bogeyman"; what an adult might call a "psychopath" or "serial killer," a child might call a "bad man." And if you're going to write about a teenager, you've got to have some of the right slang peppered through his or her dialogue or it just won't sound right to the reader. Take a look at Sample 5 for some more tips on writing dialogue.

Symbolism

Canadian literary critic and essayist Northrop Frye says we associate images of spring with comedy, summer with romance, fall with tragedy, and winter with satire or irony. So where does the horror genre fit? Well, Ray Bradbury loves to set his horror tales in October, and it is the natural month for such tales since Halloween comes at the end of it and it is the time when many life cycles are at their end — the harvest is over, the leaves are falling from the trees.

> Art is accidental; it is incidental to the writer telling his story in the best possible way he can.
>
> — J.N. WILLIAMSON

But what about other symbols? Do you need to have them in your fiction to convey a particular feeling? Yes and no. If you can slip them in without the reader noticing them, then by all means do so. But if in order to use them you have to take a wrench to the plot, stop the narrative, or do anything other than tell the story as cleanly and as clearly as possible, save your symbols for the next story or novel.

What symbols are associated with the horror genre? Goat's heads are symbols of the devil, while beetles are symbols of death, especially if one walks over your shoe! Other common symbols include such things as fire as a symbol of destruction, water as a symbol of life, and, of course, white as a color associated with goodness and black as a color associated with evil. These are all very basic. If you're truly keen on dousing your fiction with symbolism, there are many books that delve into the subject in great detail, including those that refer to the symbols associated with different cultures, such as Eastern European or Native American.

Grammar

Proper use of grammar is, of course, a necessary ingredient of good horror fiction. Certainly an author can get away with using improper grammar

sample 5
"dialogue," he said

When it comes to dialogue, there's only one word you need to know: *said.*

Many aspiring writers feel it's a writers job to use as many different words for said as there are in the English language, and in fact, books and pamphlets listing these words can be purchased through magazines such as *Writers Digest.* Frankly, these are a waste of time and money because when you use those other words you draw attention to them, distracting the reader from the story. Said is an invisible word and can be used over and over again without getting in the way. If you don't believe me, the next time you crack open a novel or read a short story, pay attention to how many times said is used.

Of course, you can use other words such as "asked" when a question's being asked, or "cried" when a character is crying or shouting, but more than that and a reader's eye will get bogged down in verbosity.

Remember also that each line of dialogue gets its own paragraph. This helps the reader know who is speaking and will allow for paragraph after paragraph without a single said. Also, it is possible to virtually do without said if you use other ways to identify who is speaking.

For example —

"He said he would be here on time," said Mary looking at her watch.

"Has he been late like this before?" asked Bob, who was waiting with her.

"Never."

"Did he call?"

"No."

Bob looked at his watch. It was getting late. Real late. "Maybe something happened to him."

Mary looked at him with fear in her eyes. "Do you think so?"

"No," said Bob. "Of course not. I'm sure he's just running late."

"Maybe." Mary sounded very unconvinced.

Just then the phone rang.

"I'll get it," said Bob.

"Would you, please."

EXERCISE 1

Write a conversation between two characters, using said as often as you like. Then go through the conversation again, taking out a few saids, and see whether or not the conversation loses any of its clarity. Then try different ways to identify who is speaking, remembering that the goal is to make the scene as clear to the reader as possible.

EXERCISE 2

Write a conversation between three or more characters, using what you've learned in the previous exercise, making it clear to the reader who is speaking at all times without interrupting the flow of normal conversation.

EXERCISE 3

Take one of the previous conversations and interject some body language to the dialogue. Then add some mention of scenery to help dramatize the scene. For example —

> "Has he been late like this before?" asked Bob, who was waiting with her.
>
> Mary looked at her watch for a long time, then shook her head. "Never."

when trying to convey a certain character's point of view: an uneducated narrator, or perhaps one from the deep south or a rural area whose word construction and phrasing is unique to the area.

It is also possible to get away with poor grammar when writing dialogue. Contrary to the quotes you read in newspaper and magazine articles and the dialogue you hear in movies and on television and read in fiction, people do not speak in grammatically correct sentences. Their speech is usually quite choppy, fragmented, and is interspersed with plenty of "Uh-uhs," and "You knows."

Finally, writers are also able to get away with ungrammatical sentences when they are trying to achieve a certain rhythm or effect with the words on the page.

Here's a section from my story "Roadkill" that breaks up a perfectly good sentence to heighten the impact when the speeding car slams into a zombie:

> *Cal looked hurt for a moment, but quickly resumed his giggling once he looked ahead and saw that they were seconds from impact.*
>
> *"Holy shit!" Cal said.*
>
> *The Cuda slammed into the zombie —*
>
> *WHAM!*
>
> *— breaking the dead thing in two.*

And here is a passage from my story "Scream String" in which short, ungrammatical sentences are used to heighten the feeling of confusion among the band members and people on stage, as well as bring out the inner madness of Johnny, who has just killed his wife by strangling her with a guitar string:

> *Nobody knew a thing.*
>
> *Except for John.*
>
> *The scream had a familiar sound to it. It was the same sound Jill had made when he'd killed her. Her death scream had been captured on the thin steel guitar string as clearly as if it had been recorded on tape.*

He ran downstage to his wah-wah pedal and pushed back on it. Nothing happened. He kicked it, but the terrible scream would not die.

One by one, the band stopped playing until all that could be heard was the scream.

Then that died as well.

And the Coliseum was silent, as if it were empty.

Johnny killed me!

Now, while I've made a case for the periodic use of ungrammatical sentences, every new writer should have a grounding in the basics of proper grammar. To explain them all here would take more room than I can afford, and besides that, good grammar isn't something specific to the horror genre; it's a universal requirement of good writing. If you're still unconvinced, just remember that Picasso could render realistic paintings as well as Norman Rockwell could but decided to use his brushes and canvas differently. Once again, know what the rules are and how to follow them before you try breaking them.

The best book on the subject of grammar is *The Elements of Style* by William Strunk Jr. and E. B. White. It's usually referred to simply as Strunk and White, and it's available in just about every bookstore on the planet.

Who's the Monster Here, Anyway?

One very effective technique for creating terror is to keep the monster offstage throughout the story. Never allow the monster to be fully seen or described by anyone, but rather only referred to by other characters.

This method has been used in a few recent situation comedies to some effect, most recently with Dr. Niles Crane's wife, Maris, on *Frasier*, and before that with Norm's wife, Vera, on *Cheers*. Over the course of the each show's run, a rather vivid character has been created without ever having that character on stage. The nonexistence of these two characters is, of course, played for laughs, but the offscreen character can be used as a source of terror.

In the horror genre, the same technique was used in the film *The Blair Witch Project*. The witches are never seen, but seeing the fear they could instill in people and knowing the devastation they could cause is more than enough to create a vivid and frightening picture in the minds of the audience.

In prose fiction, H.P. Lovecraft's "The Outsider," is the most famous story to use this technique. The monster is never seen, and the terror is created through the other characters' reactions to the monster's appearance. Quite effective.

Finally, one can't conclude a section on monsters without mentioning the classic *Twilight Zone* episode "The Monsters Are Out on Elm Street," in which a group of neighbors come out of their houses in search of an alien, ready to destroy it because it is different than they are. The alien, or "monster," is never seen, but over the course of the episode it becomes apparent that there is no monster and the only true monsters in the story are the ones bent on destroying something they don't quite understand.

A simple rule to remember when describing your monster might be that less is more. You can sometimes get more terror out of a twig snapping in the shadows of the forest than you can with a wide open mouth full of slime and razor-sharp teeth.

Jump Tales

Jump tales are the sort of stories you read (or tell) around a campfire. To scare the reader, they rely on a shock at their endings, a shock strong enough to elicit a few gasps or shrieks of terror.

One of my favorite jump tales is "The Ravine" by Ray Bradbury, in which two women are walking home from a night at the movies. They're on edge because a killer is loose in the city and has been murdering women. They walk together, the first woman getting home safely, followed by a tense, short walk alone by the other woman, who also arrives home safely. She gets all the way up to her room and breathes a sigh of relief, only to realize that there is a man inside the room with her, whom she hears when he clears his throat.

Gasp! End of story.

A jump tale. Effective, but difficult to do well unless you have a sure hand and know where the story is going and how fast you should get there.

Just Deserts

Just Deserts stories have been mentioned previously in chapter 5 in the section "Unsympathetic characters," because in a Just Deserts story it is not necessary for the main character to be likable or sympathetic. In fact, it is desirable to make the main character as nasty and despicable as possible so that when he or she dies a horrible death at the end, the reader actually cheers the character's demise and mutters, "Serves 'em right."

Going over the Top

Even Stephen King has admitted that every once in a while he's gone for the gross-out, meaning that he has described things in such revolting detail as to make a reader's stomach turn. Nothing wrong with that — the gross-out is yet another staple of the horror genre.

However, most guidelines from horror magazines and book publishers have lines that read something like, "No unnecessary violence or gore," which means that the editors don't want to see any blood and guts unless it's important to the story. Of course, you as the writer are the one who ultimately decides what's necessary and unnecessary for your story. Just be aware that not every horror fan out there thinks extreme violence and buckets of blood are cool.

7
young adult horror

Young adult (YA) and juvenile horror are two of the hottest genres in publishing today, but of late they seem to be slipping in popularity. Two signposts point to this. One is that sales of the *Goosebumps* books have been diminishing slightly over the last couple of years and R.L. Stine has announced that he won't be writing any more titles in the series. The other is that *Animorphs,* a science fiction series, has become the top seller among the younger readers. Perhaps the horror glut of the 1980s was mirrored by the YA horror glut of the 1990s. But even if sales are declining slightly, there are still many YA horror novels published each month. I myself edited a YA horror anthology for Tundra Books (a division of McClelland & Stewart) called *Be Afraid! Horrifying Stories Selected by Edo van Belkom*. The point I'm making, is that Tundra, a publisher of children's books, is just about to publish its first true horror title. There are still publishers out there who are opening up to horror, now and in the future.

When the market was thriving, many writers of adult horror tried to create series for young readers. For a number of reasons, few actually succeeded. The biggest misconception is that it is somehow easier to write a novel for young readers than it is to write a novel for adults. In fact, it is actually as difficult for a writer of adult horror to write for young adults as it is for a horror writer to suddenly jump ship and dive into the romance field. What is required is research, which means reading. If you read 100 *Goosebumps* books, chances are you'll be able to write one of your own. Same goes for the other YA series. If you want to write for the young adult market, start by reading the books that are published as YA titles.

Real Kids in Real Trouble

The first thing that sets YA fiction apart from adult fiction is that the heroes are young adults. But that doesn't mean that they have to be any less complex than the main character of an adult story. They can have just as many problems as adults have, but these must be problems particular to young people, such as a lack of acceptance by other kids. Sounds easy enough, but how are those problems conveyed to the reader?

One of the most difficult things about writing YA horror is getting your fictional young people to sound like real young people. That doesn't mean just making their dialogue genuine, but also making sure that they look at the world with hope, dreams, and aspirations that are a perfect match to their age level. This is far harder to explain than it is to recognize, so if you want to read a story in which the author got things right, try the opening novella, "Low Men in Yellow Coats," in Stephen King's collection *Hearts in Atlantis*. King has drawn a perfect portrait of an 11-year-old boy who, in one short summer, makes an all-too-quick transition from childhood to adulthood and never looks back. What's fascinating about the growth of the character Bobby Garfield is how things that seemed wonderful when he was a boy suddenly seem childish after he's received a hard kick from the real (and unreal) world. While not necessarily a YA book, this story is a good portrait of all the facets of childhood and a good model to which any YA author should aspire.

So if you've got real kids, you need things that real kids might be afraid of, things that young readers have feared at some point in their lives. Monsters are always scary, but they pale in comparison to the old man who lives down the street, the bully who lives up the street, a teacher who's not quite right, or parents who suddenly seem somehow different. These are the mainstay of YA horror because they come from the wellspring of fears experienced by young adults every day of their lives.

When you write about young adults, make them as real as you can, and when you need to give them a fright, make sure it's something young readers find frightening, something in their world that they can recognize. There's no better substitute for the feeling that *it could happen to me*.

Cliff-Hangers and Suspense

Pick up and read any *Goosebumps* title and you'll likely notice that each chapter ends with a cliff-hanger. This isn't exactly a new technique, but it is one that is quite popular in YA horror. The reason is simple: If you stop a chapter on a cliff-hanger, the reader will keep reading to learn what happens next. Sometimes the effort to ensure each chapter ends with a cliff-hanger makes the chapter ending a bit silly (a character thinks he's discovered a severed head, but it's only a bowling ball — phew!), but the technique is well worth learning.

Another thing that YA horror does is stretch out the suspense. This is good advice no matter what you're writing, but it's especially important in YA horror. Say your character has heard some noise in the basement of an old abandoned house and is on his way down to investigate. Make each step seem to take forever, and put in a few other weird noises along the way. Then, just as he's reaching the bottom of the stairs, have one of the steps break. He screams, then there's nothing but silence, even more still and ominous than before.

Once you've got the reader's attention, don't let go of it until you're good and ready to do so.

A Wholesome Theme (Do the Right Thing)

Young adult author Monica Hughes says she never starts a book with a theme in mind because if she does, she will be tempted to be a little too didactic and preachy about the theme and it will end up interfering with the story.

Say you wanted to write a young-adult horror novel on the theme of the injustice of racial prejudice. You have to be careful not to stand up on your soapbox and give one of your characters a speech about why racism is a bad thing. Instead, you've got to illustrate the point with a storyline that's interesting to the reader and with characters who do the

A Few Words With...

Mike Ford

on young adult horror

EDO VAN BELKOM: You've written in so many different genres. What special challenges does young adult horror present to a writer that other genres don't?

MIKE FORD: For me, the challenge is to create stories and characters that kids will love to read about. Readers want to feel that the story they're reading could happen to them. When I write horror or dark fantasy, I imagine what would thrill me and scare me if I were the kid it was happening to. Then I try to recreate that experience for the readers. With horror, there is also the challenge of trying to do something different. There are too many formulaic vampire/werewolf/ghost stories out there. When I write horror, I want to make it new and unusual. I want readers to feel that they've gone on an adventure. The other challenge is that YA books are now using less description and more dialogue/action. It's almost like writing a film script sometimes. So for me, it's a challenge to create atmosphere while retaining the streamlined feel that readers like.

EDO VAN BELKOM: Young adult horror has dealt with some very serious themes in recent years, but are there still subject areas that publishers are uncomfortable with?

MIKE FORD: The comfort level of publishers really goes up and down with the overall mood of the market. Most hardcover books for young adults will be sold to the school and library market. Therefore, publishers tailor their books to the comfort level of the librarians who buy them. Most librarians are really wonderful, open people, and they know that books that challenge are good for readers. But sometimes publishers will avoid certain subjects because, for whatever reason, librarians aren't willing to buy books about those subjects. But that can change very quickly, so I always tell writers to write what they want to write about and let the market take care of itself. For example, books about kids who go on killing sprees are not going to sell right now because of the extensive violence we're seeing in schools.

When it comes to paperbacks, most of those sales are made directly to readers, so it's easier to get away with "risky" issues in paperback books. For example, the Christopher Pike books frequently featured kids who killed and other kinds of traditionally taboo subjects. There's also the phenomenon — and this is not limited to YA books by any means — of more respected, established authors being able to get away with things that new writers might not be able to. It depends upon how the material is presented.

EDO VAN BELKOM: Many adult horror writers have tried to write for young adults and failed. What are some common misconceptions about the YA market?

MIKE FORD: The biggest misconception about the YA market is that it is somehow easier to write for young readers than it is to write for adults. Many adult writers think it would be fun or easy to write for kids. It isn't. They try, and they fail because they write down to their audience. They think young readers are less sophisticated than adults are. Well, the average adult bestseller is written at about a fifth-grade reading level. So there's really no need to try writing down at all. Kids want good stories with compelling characters and intriguing plots. They want to be entertained and challenged, just like adults do. If someone wants to write for young readers, they should worry less about writing down and more about writing great books.

Mike Ford is the author of numerous books for adults and young readers. A contributor to the Spinetinglers _series of horror novels, he is best known as the primary author of the_ Eerie Indiana _series of novels, featuring characters from the television show of the same name._

right thing, not because they must to be in keeping with the book's theme, but because that is what they would do in that specific situation.

This is not to say that characters in YA fiction can't behave badly. But if they do, then they must face the consequences of their actions, just like all the badasses in adult horror stories.

If you want to send a message, write a letter or pick up the phone. If you try to give a sermon in your fiction, young readers will sense they're being lectured to and will tune out, just like real kids do when you try to tell them something for their own good.

Humor

Humor is a great device for pacing, and young readers like a laugh just as much as adults do. But remember that what's funny to an adult isn't so to a youngster. A recent trip to the theater to see *Inspector Gadget* illustrated this point for me perfectly. While my son howled throughout the movie, I barely cracked a smile. He'd laugh himself silly each time a character's pants would fall down, but I laughed only once, when Gadget woke up from his extensive surgery, tried to get out of bed, and, of course, fell flat on his face. This was funny to me because I've been through a few surgeries and know exactly what it's like to wake up totally disoriented and uncoordinated. My son, on the other hand, without much in the way of personal reference on the subject, barely giggled.

In a horror story, humor is sort of like having the characters all sitting around having a coffee break. It's used to give readers a break too, so they'll be rested when it comes time for more scary bits.

For example, back in the section Cliff-Hangers and Suspense, we had our character go down into the basement to check out a noise. He takes each step slowly, hearing each step creak and moan beneath his feet. Then, just before he reaches the bottom, a step breaks and he screams. Then silence, and he realizes he's just had a good scare and starts to laugh. And as he's laughing, a big hairy hand with sharp claws shoots out of the darkness to grab him.

Suspense. Humor. Boo!

> Humor and horror both invoke a reaction by means of shock and/or surprise. Both make effective use of the same element — the unexpected. I use either in order to startle the reader; I find this helps keep him awake.
>
> — ROBERT BLOCH

Does Everybody Get out Alive?

Although each YA publisher will have its own rules regarding violence in the books it publishes, keep in mind that the younger your target audience, the less violent the story can be.

For example, in just about every *Goosebumps* book, the kids who get into trouble at the beginning of the book usually get out of trouble by the end, often without a scratch. They save themselves through the use of their own wit and courage. Sometimes other characters — villains who weren't on their best behavior — end up having something bad happen to them by the end of the story, but mostly they are not killed off or hurt too badly. They might be in a jam, but there's a sense that they'll get out of it later, either on their own or with someone else's help.

Titles for older young readers allow more leeway on the subject. If a novel is geared toward young adults — early teenagers — there's a good chance that not all the characters who are there at the start of the book will be there at the end.

The best advice on the subject of violence is to read a few titles from different publishers and find out firsthand what's allowed and what isn't.

The Evil Can (and Will) Return

Having the evil defeated but not totally wiped out is a staple of the horror genre, especially of YA horror. When the kids get out of the haunted house alive, they haven't gotten rid of the evil within it; they've only escaped it. The ordeal they've just come through will be happening to some other kids before long. Or the evil they've bested is gone now, but will be back in another 10, 50, or 100 years, and the heroes of this story must live with the knowledge that their sons and daughters will have to deal with it some day too.

This way of ending a YA story lends itself to a sequel or a series of stories. If *Monster Blood* couldn't be tamed in the number 3 book of the *Goosebumps* series, perhaps it could be in the number 18 book, *Monster Blood II*, or the number 29 book, *Monster Blood III*.

The evil always returns, sometimes in the form of monster blood, sometimes in some other form — but it always comes back.

Don't Dumb It Down

Young adult horror author Richard Lee Byers calls this a "Five-D Don't": Don't Dare Deliberately Dumb it Down.

By that he means that under no circumstances should you change concepts or even phrasing because you think that young readers won't understand. Just as young readers will know when you're lecturing them, they will also know when you're talking down to them. It's better for young readers to come across a word they don't understand (which might encourage them to ask an adult what the word means or even go look it up in the dictionary) than to feel as if they're reading a *Dick and Jane* book.

8
Revising and polishing

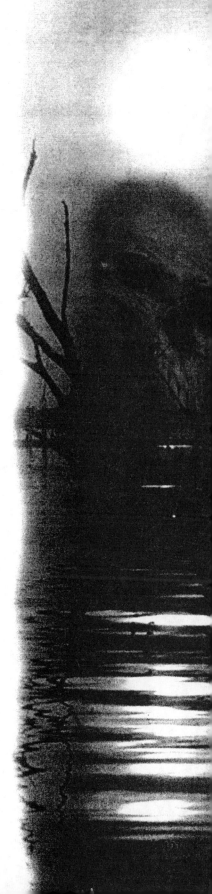

Revising and polishing your work to make it the absolute best it can possibly be is one of the easiest ways to become a better writer, but it is also one of the most difficult things to get a new writer to do. After all, once you've completed a story and checked it for spelling and grammar, how much more can there be to do? The answer is plenty.

Have you used the best words and phrases to describe things or were you satisfied simply with good words? Is there a slight glitch in your story that you think no one will notice? Is there a detail you've left out because you didn't want to make a trip to the library to do the research to get it right?

All this is part of revising and polishing your work to make sure it is the best that it can be.

Revising

Revising can be a difficult task for the aspiring writer. You've spent so much time on your story and novel, how could you possibly change any of it, or even worse, cut something out?

The truth is, even the work of the best writers of the day can be improved by revision and cutting. But if you're still learning how to *write* a story, how and where are you going to learn how to *revise* it?

It used to be that magazine editors were good people from whom to get advice on how to revise your story and make it salable. Book editors also used to have more input into a book prior to publication, asking for revisions and changes several times before ushering it into print. Today, if a book isn't close to being publishable as is, an editor won't likely spend the time working with an author to fix it. That job now seems to rest solely on the author's shoulders.

Most editors are too busy these days to offer more than a scribbled note along with a rejection slip, and that's only if you're lucky. So if editors aren't about to provide you with suggestions, who is?

Getting second and third opinions

It never hurts to get a second opinion about your work, but if you're asking the wrong person for advice, it might hurt you more than you think it will. I've always said that you should never ask your husband, wife, mother, father, brother, lover, or close personal friend what he or she thinks of your work. Furthermore, you shouldn't ask anyone who has an interest in your personal well-being. What you don't want is someone telling you something you wrote was good because he or she doesn't want to hurt your feelings (husband, wife), or because his or her eyes are clouded by affection and pride in your effort (mother, father).

The right person to give you advice is someone who can be absolutely honest, who doesn't care if the truth hurts your feelings, who has read in the field in which you're writing, and who knows how to articulate his or her thoughts. A tall order certainly, but not an impossible one. If you work in an office, find out who reads books on breaks at lunch hour, and then ask if he or she might like to give you feedback on your story.

This is an important part of writing and selling fiction. The time you want to hear criticism of your work is before you've sent it to an editor, because once it's in the editor's hands you can't make any more changes to it until the editor's made a decision on it.

And if you think that at some point you'll no longer need the advice of others, think again. A good friend of mine who has published 12 novels to date and won countless major awards still gets a dozen or so people to read each of his novels before he turns them in to his editor.

My own first critique was at the hands of respected SF author Judith Merril, who absolutely savaged my attempts at writing an SF novel and left me walking around with my tail between my legs for days. But I bounced back, wrote more crap, and eventually produced something salable. Years later, Merril told me that she thought I had talent (although I couldn't write very good science fiction), but she wasn't about to tell me that at the time and watch me get a swelled head. Nevertheless, she was there at the launch party for my first novel and proud to have played a part in my education as a writer.

This all refers back to one of the underlying messages of this book: Writing is hard work. If you're not prepared for honest criticism and rejection of your work, perhaps you'd be better suited to some other profession.

Letting a story simmer for a while

Once you've finished a story you're likely going to be proud of it and eager to show it around. A word of advice: *Don't.*

When you've finished a story or novel, pat yourself on the back for a job well done, put the story in a drawer, and let it sit for a few days (if you're in a hurry) or a few weeks or months while you work on your next masterpiece. When you read the story over again several weeks later, you'll be looking at it with fresh eyes, and you'll be able to notice things that you couldn't see before because you were all too familiar with the story, having worked on it steadily for so long.

Things such as spelling mistakes and bad grammar become more apparent after a break because you're not as familiar with the text as you were when you were working on it. For the same reason, awkward and run-on sentences will also seem to be more obvious to you, as will gaps in logic, poor dialogue, and the need for more detail. If you let it sit long enough, it will be almost as if you're reading it for the first time, just like your readers.

Tightening

Aspiring writers often have trouble cutting parts from their own work. That's because it took so much effort to write in the first place that it's painful to see it go. But every single word you write doesn't necessarily belong in the story you're working on at the moment. If you cut something from a novel (say a scene or a chapter), you can always save it and later on turn it into a short story or part of another novel.

Here's an example of the kind of tightening stories can go through. The paragraph is from my first short story, "Baseball Memories," which was originally published in 1989, then reprinted in *Year's Best Horror Stories XX* and several other places since then. But even after several reprintings and some ten years, the story can still benefit from a bit of tightening.

Original published version

> *Sam had a memory like most people when it came to regular things. He forgot the odd birthday or anniversary now and then, but no one ever thought him to be anything more than slightly absentminded.*

With some tightening

> *Sam had a memory like most when it came to regular things. He forgot the odd birthday or anniversary but no one ever thought he was anything more than absentminded.*

During my time as an aspiring writer, a moment in which I thought that I might someday be a real writer came when I discarded a large section of a story I was working on and tried a completely different tack. What was important to me at that moment was the quality of the work, not just doing the work, and I felt as if I was that much better a writer (all right, an aspiring writer) because of it.

Some writers and editors say you have to be ruthless with your own work, cutting and slashing until the work is as taut as a drumhead. Realistically speaking, things aren't so bad. Just remember that sometimes material needs to be cut from a work in order for it to be improved (like the 100,000-word section — the equivalent of a very large novel — of Stephen King's *The Stand* that was cut from the book for its original publication in 1978, then added to the book for its reissue in 1990).

Polishing

When you've spent some six months, or maybe even six years working on a novel, it often becomes a burden to look at the same words one more time. But polishing a work of prose until you've worked out all its kinks is probably one of the best things you can do for yourself. Remember, once you've sent it off, you can't fix it any more.

In order to be a good writer, you must first explode passionately and then render it down. It's always best to do the big thing initially and then cut it down to size. Every time I write a story, I'll do about 30 pages and then pare it down to around 20.

— RAY BRADBURY

But when you've got the story or novel working as well as you possibly can and you don't know what's left to fix, pick scenes or chapters at random and read them over. Skip from front to back, reading a few pages here and there, and see if it's all as good as you remember it being. Read a section out loud and see how it *sounds* as opposed to how it *looks* on the page. Quite often, mistakes are more apparent when heard rather than read. If you catch just a single mistake, the entire exercise will have been worth it.

Proofreading

Proofreading is one of the easiest ways to polish your manuscript. While the spell checkers on computers are good tools for catching some misspelled words, they should never, under any circumstances, be used as the only or final check of your spelling.

The reason for this is simple.

Everyone else on the planet will tell you that you shouldn't trust spell checkers because they can't tell the difference between "their," "there," and "they're," but I have a more dramatic example. Don't trust your computer's spell checker because it can't tell the difference between the following two words:

therapist

the rapist

And proofreading is just a plain good idea if you want to submit to professional markets and look like a pro in print. For years I had a sign in front of my computer screen that read **PROOFREAD** in big black letters. It was a reminder to me that as much as I didn't want to read through a story yet again, it was something that had to be done. If I were competing against ten other writers for a spot in an anthology or magazine, I figured that I could easily improve the quality of my story just by reading it for typos one more time. Nothing reflects more poorly on a writer than a typo that could easily have been caught if only the writer had been more careful.

I took the sign down several years ago, but the proofreading habit has stayed with me, and I've often been complemented on how clean and well prepared my manuscripts are.

One last read through

And now that you've got everything polished and clean, take one last look at the manuscript — as much as it might pain you to do so — reading it over in hard copy, where words and phrases look different from the way they do on-screen. You might find something you didn't see before now — a typo, the wrong word, or an out-of-place comma.

This is, after all, your very last chance to make a correction, and you had better take it. There's nothing more disconcerting to a writer than seeing a typo in a manuscript just as it's going into the envelope. It makes you wonder, "If I just saw that one, how many others might there be?"

You'll sleep better, and have a better chance of making a sale, if the issue never comes up and you're unable to find any problems at all.

part three
the horror marketplace

It only took ten years, seven unpublished novels, and a lot of
blood later before I sold *The Wolfen*.

— WHITLEY STRIEBER

I would also say: never give up. I once had a story rejected 72
times; it took me six and a half years to sell it. But I did. It's like
going to a party where there are 60 people. You can't expect to
please all of them. But if you can just meet the right one, then
you can forget the others you never connected with.

— DENNIS ETCHISON

9 SELLING HORROR

You've just finished writing a horror story that's so scary it gives even you the creeps.

But while the satisfaction of having written a fine story is a great feeling, if you're like most writers, you probably want to share your work with as many readers as possible.

Ah, but where to send it to achieve that goal?

It's a popular question for new writers, one that ranks right up there with such classics as "Where do you get your ideas?" and "How do I find an agent?"

Marketing Your Short Fiction

The conventional wisdom on marketing short stories, whether they be horror genre or mainstream, tells you to create a list of the best-paying markets and submit to each of them from the top down, sending the story to the most lucrative market first. If and when the story is rejected, you immediately send it to the second most lucrative magazine, gradually working your way down the list until the story finally sells.

Unfortunately, there aren't the same kind of high-paying, prestigious markets in the horror field as there are in, say, science fiction and fantasy. Horror currently has nothing comparable to magazines such as *Asimov's* or *Science Fiction Age,* established magazines that both pay well and have a high circulation. There were several top-flight horror magazines publishing in the mid-1980s, such as *Night Cry* and *Twilight Zone,* but sadly those magazine are no more.

However, despite the demise of some top horror markets, there are still several highly regarded magazines publishing horror. A recent *Writer's Digest* Fiction 50 — an annual list of the top 50 magazines publishing fiction in the United States — included 3 "horror" magazines. *The Urbanite* was ranked number 22, *2 AM* was ranked number 23, and *Worlds of Fantasy and Horror* (now called *Weird Tales* once again) came in at number 50. (See Sample 6 for a partial list of the 1999 Fiction 50 magazines.)

It's important to note that the markets included in the Fiction 50 list are judged on a number of criteria, from rate of pay to the number of stories published in a year, from providing personalized rejections to having a broad range of interest. Therefore, some highly regarded (albeit low-paying or low-circulation) magazines in the horror genre did not make the list.

These magazines are known as semi-professional and small-press magazines. Some very prestigious horror magazines such as *Cemetery Dance* and *Dark Regions* are considered to be semi-professional, but have nevertheless published some of the best short fiction in the field to date. For example, Jack Ketchum's short story "The Box," first published in *Cemetery Dance,* won the 1994 Bram Stoker Award for best short story.

Market Information

So, if there are horror markets out there, how do you find out about them? (Another often-asked question.)

Fortunately, the horror genre is blessed with many excellent sources of market information, covering everything from small-press magazines to anthologies from major publishers.

The best of the lot is *Scavenger's Newsletter,* which has been published monthly by writer Janet Fox for more than ten years. Each issue contains timely information on new markets, updated guidelines for established markets, and all sorts of market news shared by writers who are regularly submitting to the magazines.

sample 6
writer's digest fiction 50

Below are the entries under Magazines Publishing Speculative Fiction (Science Fiction, Fantasy, and Horror) that appeared in the 1999 *Writer's Digest* Fiction 50, a list of the top 50 markets for short fiction in North America.

4. *The Magazine of Fantasy and Science Fiction*
    Gordon Van Gelder, editor
    PO Box 1806
    New York, NY 10159-1806

6. *Isaac Asimov's Science Fiction Magazine*
    Gardner Dozois, editor
    475 Park Avenue South, 11th Floor
    New York, NY 10016

10. *The Urbanite: Surreal & Lively & Bizarre*
    Mark McLaughlin, editor
    PO Box 4737
    Davenport, IA 52808

12. *Analog Science Fiction and Fact*
    Stanley Schmidt, editor
    475 Park Avenue South, 11th Floor
    New York, NY 1001

37. *Marion Zimmer Bradley's Fantasy Magazine*
    PO Box 249
    Berkeley, CA 94701-0249

Another worthwhile publication is the *Gila Queen's Guide to Markets*. Published on an infrequent schedule by Katherine Ptacek (wife of author Charles L. Grant and a fine horror writer in her own right), each issue of this newsletter focuses on a specific genre — romance, westerns, mystery, erotica — in addition to providing up-to-date information about new and established markets.

These newsletters are invaluable if you have several stories to market or if you feel more comfortable breaking into the horror field at the ground level and slowly working your way up to the professional ranks.

Selling to the Small Press

If you've sent your story to all the top markets without any luck or have been discouraged by countless impersonal rejection slips, you might consider sending your story to some lower-paying markets or even those that pay in contributor's copies.

Small-press magazines can be an excellent starting point, for several reasons. First, there are many small-press horror magazines, most of which are eager to publish new writers. Second, the contact you have with editors is quite often on a more personal level than can be had with editors at the top magazines. Finally, making a sale, even to a pays-in-copies magazine, can give you some much-needed confidence as you work toward more professional markets.

That's how it worked for me.

My first story, "Baseball Memories," was published in a pays-in-copies literary magazine called *Aethlon*. After the story appeared there, it was selected by Karl Edward Wagner for the 20th installment of his *Year's Best Horror* anthology series.

Luckily for me, that story found its own top market. However, *Aethlon* was not the first place I sent the story; it was the fourth, after it had been rejected by some of the top magazines of the day. Would it have sold to a top market if I had continued to use the "top down" method of marketing? Perhaps, but selling to small-press magazines, with the occasional submission to the top markets of a story I thought had some merit, seemed the best route for me early in my career.

Cracking the Pro Markets

It must be stressed, though, that while the small press is a great place to learn the craft of writing, it is not a place to forge out a professional

A Few Words With...

Kathryn Ptacek

on markets for horror fiction

EDO VAN BELKOM: How have the markets for horror fiction changed in the last ten years?

KATHRYN PTACEK: The field is not as strong as it used to be. A decade ago the horror boom was on — everyone, it seemed, was publishing horror novels. And that meant that a lot of really bad — along with the really good — manuscripts were being purchased by the New York publishing houses. You don't have that now. Many publishers no longer purchase horror novels, or they look for it in another guise — "dark suspense," etc. As for magazines, there never have been many professionally paying horror markets, but over the years there have been many more small-press zines showing up. There are also a lot of smaller publishing houses now doing books, companies that weren't around ten years ago, or even five.

EDO VAN BELKOM: What area of horror fiction do you see growing fastest in the next ten years?

KATHRYN PTACEK: Good question. I don't know. If I did, I'd probably be hard at work writing it now. I don't think we'll ever see horror booming the way we did back in the 80s. But I think now there might be a real resurgence of "quiet" horror; that is, stuff that's not gory, that just sort of creeps up on you — ghost and witch stuff, for instance.

EDO VAN BELKOM: Where would a new writer have the best chance of publication?

KATHRYN PTACEK: If a new writer wants to get published more easily (I'm not saying it's easy, though), she might try a small press publication. However, I always maintain that a writer should start with the top market, and then work her way down. Sometimes, though, it's nice to get that publishing credit, even if it's a low-paying market.

Kathryn Ptacek, also known as the Gila Queen, is the publisher of the Gila Queen's Guide to Markets, *a guide to markets and all sorts of publishing information and tips for writers and artists. She is the author of numerous novels, among them* Shadoweyes *and* In Silence Sealed, *and has also published numerous short stories, reviews, and articles.*

horror-writing career. Although the small press represents a large market for horror fiction, many of the publications operate on very shaky ground in terms of financing and personnel. Small-press magazines frequently fold after a single issue, or will sometimes hold onto stories for years before deciding not to print another issue — often without notifying the story's author!

This kind of aggravation is one of the reasons why some horror writers spend only a few years publishing in the small press before making the move up to the pro ranks. (Of my first 50 short story sales, 17 went to small-press markets, but out of each group of 10 stories that were published, 7, 5, 4, and 1 story in 10 appeared in small-press magazines, with the rest going to professional magazines and anthologies.) The trade-off is that while you still might be frustrated by rejection slips from the better magazines, at least you'll know that when a story is accepted, it will in fact end up being published.

Access to information about purely professional markets is one advantage of joining a pro writers' organization such as the Horror Writers Association (HWA). As well as providing new writers with an opportunity to make contacts within the field and learn from established pros, each HWA newsletter includes listings for horror markets paying professional word rates for fiction. As a bonus, some of these markets — such as the 1995 anthologies *100 Wicked Little Witch Stories* and *100 Vicious Little Vampire Stories* — are open exclusively to HWA members.

Of course, being a professional writers' organization, HWA concerns itself only with professionally paying horror markets. Science Fiction Writers Association (SFWA) is interested in professionally paying science fiction and fantasy markets, while in Canada, Science Fiction Canada concerns itself with markets that pay both professional and semi-professional word rates.

Mainstream Markets for Horror

But what if the semi-professional magazines all rejected your story and you're not keen on seeing it printed in the small press? What do you do then?

The answer is simple: Try submitting it to mainstream or other non-horror markets.

Obviously, some mainstream markets like *Redbook* or *Ladies' Home Journal* won't be very receptive to stories about zombies, ghouls, and vampires, but some other top magazines might. For example, the *Magazine of Fantasy and Science Fiction*, number 9 in the last Fiction 50, sometimes publishes horror stories, and contemporary horror often finds its way onto the pages of *Alfred Hitchcock's Mystery Magazine*, listed 25th out of 50.

But many professional magazines outside of the top 50 will also consider horror fiction. For years, the slick men's magazine *Cavalier* routinely published the horror fiction of Stephen King, Dennis Etchison, and Mort Castle. Sadly, *Cavalier* is no more, but there are still countless other magazines that will consider publishing a horror tale if it conforms with the overall needs of the magazine.

I once read a posting on an electronic bulletin board about a magazine for truckers called *RPM*. The posting mentioned that the magazine published fiction, and that got me thinking. Since any story appearing in the magazine would obviously have to be about trucks and/or trucking, I wondered if they might be interested in a story of mine called "Death Drives a Semi." As it turned out, they were interested in the story, even if it was horror, paying me five cents a word, eight contributors copies, and an *RPM* baseball cap for one-time rights. To top it all off, the magazine had a circulation of 120,000.

It doesn't get much better than that.

Study and Know the Horror Market

Sales like that don't happen all the time, but they are possible if you keep your ears and eyes open and study the market.

One excellent source for finding alternative horror markets is the annual *Novel and Short Story Writer's Market* published by Writer's Digest Books. Each year the *Novel and Short Story Writer's Market* lists hundreds of professional, literary, and small-press magazines and journals, as well as contests, agents, and book publishers. You'll have to spend some time studying the listings to find the ones that will consider horror, but once you do you'll have a great list of markets to which you can submit your stories.

There's another tried and true method of finding markets for your horror, or any other type of story you might want to sell. It's called first-hand market research and it's done at your local newsstand or bookstore.

Say yours is a literary horror story, heavy on atmosphere and mood. You might want to take a look at several of the literary magazines on the shelf and give them a try. And if your horror story features a serial killer, you might try sending it to a mystery or crime magazine. And if you can't make up your mind about which of the magazines you want to submit to, there's no better way to determine what kind of fiction a magazine publishes than by buying a copy and reading it from cover to cover.

This last point you've probably heard before, but it's something that bears repeating because —

The best way to market your short fiction is to know your short fiction markets.

10 manuscript format

So you feel you've written a pretty good horror story, done some market research, and found a couple of magazines that publish the type of story you've just written. Now you're ready to print up the story and send it off to a magazine so you can find out what an honest-to-goodness editor thinks of it. Great — but there's just one more thing you need to do before you send the story through the printer, and that's make sure the story is in proper manuscript format.

Looking Like a Pro in Print

How important can formatting be? I mean, it's the story that counts, right?

Absolutely, but to have the editor read the story and judge it solely on its own merits, you need to present it in the proper format so the editor isn't distracted by the format and can concentrate solely on the content.

It can sometimes be difficult to get this concept across to a new writer. Once, when I was teaching a college creative writing course and explaining that each new paragraph had to be indented, a student called me on it saying that in business letters paragraphs are never indented. In another class, a student's word processor had printed the last line of each page twice, once at the bottom of the page and again at the top of the next. The student blamed her computer, then refused to believe an editor would reject a story because of the mistake.

Maybe, maybe not. Be aware that editors spend much more of their time rejecting stories than accepting them, and anything that makes the job of rejecting a story easier means one less manuscript the editor has to read all the way to the end. Chances are that a writer who hasn't bothered to learn something as easy as how to format a manuscript properly hasn't learned how to do all those other neat things like tell a good story, flesh out characters, and build suspense.

The Basics of Manuscript Format

The good thing about manuscript format is that it is easy to learn, and once learned, is never forgotten. Many books on writing explain what proper manuscript format is, but few explain the reasons behind all the quirks of the format. Sample 7 is an original short story of mine called "The Morning After." The story, a short-short of less than 1,000 words, might never be confused with a work of great literature, but at least its format is exemplary.

1. The first page of the manuscript should include your name, address, and phone number, and any other way in which an editor might be able to get in touch with you. In this case I've added lines for a fax number and an e-mail address. E-mail correspondence between editors and writers has become more common in recent years, so include an e-dress if you have one.

    It's important to include all this information because an editor just might need to get in touch with you in a hurry, and the more options an editor has to do so, the more likely he or she is to connect with you. When I submitted what turned out to be my fifth short story sale, I put only my address on the first page. When the editors of *On Spec* decided to buy "The Basement" and needed to get in touch with me, they ended up calling a couple of my friends to get my phone number. I got a kick from knowing that an editor had contacted some of my writer friends and let them know that I'd sold a story to *On Spec*, but it would have been nice to be the first person to hear the good news.

sample 7
manuscript format

Edo van Belkom
1 Horror Writer Avenue
City, Province/State
COUNTRY   W3L W7T
Phone: (905) 555-3208
Fax: (905) 555-3207
E-mail: edress@emailaddress.com

①

② 800 Words

③

⑤ THE MORNING AFTER
by Edo van Belkom

⑥ He tried to open his eyes, but his eyelids were still too heavy with sleep.

Last night had left him utterly exhausted.

Correction: <u>She</u> had left him utterly exhausted.

④ She had been a gorgeous, dark-haired beauty, with tanned skin and mysterious eyes. The kind of woman he'd always dreamed about, but knew he could never have.⑦

That's because at five feet tall, slightly balding on top, and more than a couple of spare tires around the middle, Mort Broitman wasn't exactly a magnet for attractive women.

Up until last night, most of his dates had been friends of friends of his mother. But last night, she'd been all his, and he had lived a dream he'd been fantasizing about since his teens...

④

#

She met him in the bar after work. Came right up to him and introduced herself. At first he thought she'd mistaken him for someone else, but she insisted that he was the one she wanted.

After that, things seemed to move at light speed.

They ordered drinks. She laughed at his jokes. More drinks. More laughter. Then she said, "Why don't we go to my place?"

Morty's jaw nearly hit the floor, but somehow he managed to get it back in place long enough to say, "Yes."

Minutes later they were in a cab headed for her apartment.

As they rode in the cab, all Morty could think about was how this wasn't really happening to him and what on Earth could this woman — a woman who could obviously have any man she pleased — possibly want with him?

When he asked her, she laughed and assured him that he had something no other man could give her.

He was about to ask what that thing was when he caught a glimpse of her stockings and lace garters peeking out at him from beneath her skirt. Suddenly, he was past caring about the <u>why</u> and was interested only in the <u>when</u>.

He didn't have to wait long.

Seconds after they stepped through the door, she was on him like a wildwoman, tearing away his clothes and ravaging him as if he were the last man on Earth.

After that it was all a blur that lead into the bedroom where they made love and drank wine, first one then the other, long into the night.

And, as he was about to orgasm for the third time, he caught himself wondering yet again what a woman like her would want with a man like him.

The answer had to wait until morning since he followed up his climax by promptly falling into a deep, deep sleep.

⑨ #

The morning after, he felt sore all over.

He raised a hand to wipe the sleep from his eyes and he was hit by a sudden jolt of pain that burned down the right side of his body.

It almost made him cry out.

He lifted his hand again, slowly this time, and again felt a sharp pain jabbing into his side.

He tried to roll to the left, but he was stuck to the sheets — actually glued to them.

The thought of it made him queasy.

He wanted to call out for help, but realized he'd never asked her name. Besides that, he had the strange feeling he was alone in this apartment — an apartment that looked quite empty and sterile, almost like a hospital room.

He tried rolling to the right again, this time not stopping until his body was free of the sheets. Then he tried to lift himself off the bed, but the pain was so excruciating he was forced to lay back down and catch his breath.

Minutes passed. He tried again. Biting his lower lip, he fought the pain and got himself upright. Then, taking advantage of his momentum, managed to get to his feet. He walked stiffly toward the bathroom.

There he flipped on the light and looked in the mirror. <u>God, I look</u> ⑩ <u>awful,</u> he thought. His face was puffy and swollen, there were bags under his eyes, and dried drool had crusted at the corners of his mouth.

He leaned closer to the mirror.

And noticed something wrong.

The skin on his side was almost black. He turned slightly for a better look and suddenly felt the need to vomit.

His back was caked with dried blood. The blood had come from a six-inch long incision in his lower back, now sewn shut by about two dozen stitches.

Morty's mind wheeled back to the previous night and the question he'd asked himself over and over.

<u>What could this woman possibly want from me?</u> ⑩

Now the answer was painfully obvious.

One of his kidneys.

⑪ # # # # # #

Since then I've never neglected to include all my contact information on every manuscript I send out, even to editors I've been dealing with for years. Why make an editor's dealings with you any more difficult than they have to be?

2. Placing the word count on a manuscript serves a number of purposes. First of all, it tells the publisher how much he or she has to pay for the right to publish your story. For example, "The Morning After" is roughly 800 words long, and if it sold to a magazine paying 3¢ per word, payment for the story would be $24.

Another reason for putting the word count on the first page is that it identifies the story's length at a glance. Say an editor has a few pages left in the current issue of a magazine and needs a story of between 800 to 1,000 words. He or she takes a quick look through the slush pile and pulls out all the stories of that length, including yours. As a result, your story is getting some added attention that it wouldn't have received otherwise.

Now, the number of words in "The Morning After" wasn't exactly 800. According to WordStar, the program the story was written on, the word count comes to 789, a number that is easily rounded off to 800. For longer stories it's a good idea to always round down from 50 and less, and up from 51 and more. That means that a word count done by your computer of 3,242 would be shown as "3,200 Words" on the first page of the manuscript, and a count of 3,258 would become "3,300 Words." You could, of course, post the exact count provided by your word-processing program, but editors aren't concerned that your computer can count words; they want a general idea of how much space your story will take up in their magazine. Also, different word processors count words differently (some count actual words, some count the number of characters and divide by four or five, etc.), so the number you provide on the manuscript might differ significantly from the number given by the publisher's own program once the story is typeset. For that reason, and the others already mentioned, it's best to round off the count.

3. Empty white space is a useful thing for editors. That's why manuscripts should always start halfway down the first page. This leaves a large blank space at the start of the story on which an editor can write notes: notes intended as reminders to himself

or herself ("Check with publisher on subject matter"), messages to another editor or typesetter ("Do you think this will work in the upcoming organ transplant theme issue?"), or a comment on the manuscript intended for the author ("If you change it from a kidney to a lung, I'll buy it").

4. Proper manuscript format requires that you leave an inch of white space all the way around the type. This white space serves the same purpose as the white space at the top half of the first page: it gives the editor room to make notes.

5. The title of your story doesn't have to be set in capital letters, but it should be given some special distinction from the story's text so that it can be identified and read quickly and easily. Instead of capitals, you could underline the title, wrap it in quotation marks, or use a different typeface — one of the few times that a different font might be desirable.

    Including your name, as I did ("by Edo van Belkom"), is optional if the name on the byline is the same on the address in the upper left-hand corner of the page. However, including a name is recommended because it is necessary to have a name listed if you're using a pseudonym. For example, if I wanted to publish the story under the pseudonym I sometimes use, Evan Hollander, the story's title and byline would read —

    THE MORNING AFTER
by Evan Hollander

    Doing this will ensure that the story is published under the pseudonym. This change is the only one required when using a pseudonym. Just make sure your real name appears along with your address so the magazine's accounting department will know to whom the check should be made out and where to send it.

6. You should begin each new paragraph with an indent. If you're working on a word processor, you can insert an indent by hitting the tab key. If you're still working on a typewriter (and there's nothing wrong with that, especially considering that top fantasist Harlan Ellison and prolific horror novelist J.N. Williamson both still use typewriters), the typical indent is five spaces in. Do not indicate the start of a new paragraph by using a blank line space.

The text should be double-spaced, which will leave an editor enough room to make notes or corrections to your manuscript between the lines of text. This is handy for corrections of typos, imprecise words, or the rewriting of a phrase or sentence.

Finally, the font you should be using is a 10- or 12-point Courier. Many writing guides and manuals will tell you it's okay to use serif fonts such as Times Roman because they are easier to read. That may be true, but if you are following the rest of the points outlined here, there is a very specific reason for using the Courier.

If you've used Courier, double-spaced the manuscript, and left a one-inch margin around your text, then each one of your lines will be 60 to 65 characters long and have roughly 10 to 12 words to it, and each page will have about 250 words on it. That makes it easy for an editor to make a guess as to your story's length, even if you haven't put the word count in the top right-hand corner of the first page. Use of all these points also makes it easy for an editor to know how much he or she has cut from your manuscript when he or she has edited out a few paragraphs.

One thing all writing manuals agree on is that you should not use any sans serif fonts, such as Helvetica. It's terrific that your processor can produce all those wonderful fonts, but they're not for manuscripts, and over the course of a few pages will put a strain on an editor's eyes.

7. While the left-hand margin of your manuscript is justified (meaning that except for indents, all the lines start at the same point) the right-hand margin must remain ragged. This ragged edge is called ragged right. Leaving the right-hand side of the manuscript ragged ensures that all of the letters and words are equally spaced across the line. If you used a justified-right setup, your computer's word processor would squeeze some words together and stretch others apart so that each line ends at the same point. The compressing and expanding of words makes them more difficult to read, which may hinder an editor's ability to judge the work on its own merits.

Another thing to avoid on the right-hand side of the page is the use of hyphens. When words are printed in newspapers, magazines, and books, hyphens are often used to break up longer words so that at least part of the word can be used to fill out a line. That's fine for typeset text, but for manuscripts, hyphens just make things more difficult for the editor to read, and that's what you're doing all this to prevent.

8. After your name, address, and contact information appears on the first page of the manuscript, each following page should have a header on it with your name, the name of your story, and a page number. This might seem like a bit much, but imagine a young editorial assistant has picked up a pile of manuscripts from one editor's desk and is carrying them across the office to deliver them to the desk of another editor. The assistant trips on an extension cord halfway across the room and the manuscripts go flying. Your name, story title, and page number on each page will make it that much easier to put your manuscript back together again.

   If you've written a piece for a particular publication, you can also include the name of it in the header. If I had done this for the story in Sample 7, the header would have read —

   Edo van Belkom/ WRITING HORROR: The Morning After/ 2

   Doing this helps editors who work on more than one magazine or anthology at a time to know at a glance (or serves as a reminder about) the publication for which the manuscript is intended.

9. Line breaks are used to signify a change of scene, the passage of time, or a change in point of view. Some books on writing will tell you that leaving a blank line to signify a line break is acceptable, but it is not. When the blank line appears as the first or last line on a page, it is invisible and will cause the reader a moment or two of confusion.

   Some publishers' guidelines ask that you use three asterisks to signify a line break. If the guidelines ask for something specific, then follow the guidelines. If not, it's best just to use a number sign.

10. Although computers make the use of italics easy, it's still not advised for manuscripts. The best way to indicate the use of italics is to underline the words or phrases to be italicized. Underlining is the clearest, most easily discernible way to differentiate regular type from its italicized brethren. In fact, it is the best

way to indicate when any font other than the standard should be used. For example, if you have the words from a lawn sign in your story, or the headline of a newspaper article, indicate it by underlining the words. This is done because no matter what font you'd like to see used, the ultimate decision on typeface will be made by the copy editor or book designer, who will use the fonts that are standard for the magazine or publishing house.

Sometimes a character's thoughts are set in italics, which sets them apart from the rest of the text. This tactic can sometimes become unwieldy if throughout the text italics are also used for other things, such as emphasis on specific words. I used italics twice to express thought in "The Morning After," but only because it is a short-short and the italics can be used to highlight the character's thoughts without getting in the way. If the story had been any longer, I likely would have not used italics at all. This is a judgment call made by the author for each individual story or novel. The only rule is that if you use italics for a character's thoughts once, you have to use it consistently for that purpose throughout the manuscript.

11. In nonfiction work, especially articles and magazines, it is customary to place -30- at the end of the piece. There's no such tradition in fiction writing, and authors have used any number of ways to end a story, from typing *THE END* at the bottom of the last page to using a string of number signs. If your story ends on the last line of a page, then it's a good idea to let the editor know the story's over so he or she won't go looking for the next page.

If you've sold a story and have been asked to provide a disk version of it, you should delete whatever you've used to indicate the end of your story. When I sent a disk version of my story "Reaper Vs. Reaper Vs. Reaper" to White Wolf for inclusion in their anthology *Death and Damnation*, I left the words *THE END* at the end of the story. The stories in the book were published from their disk versions almost untouched, and out of 12 stories, 5 had nothing at their ends, while 4 had END, with 1 each sporting *THE END* (mine), Finis, and *(end)*. In this instance, it would have been better to have left the end of the story blank.

Other Things to Note about Manuscript Format

Listing rights

Some books on writing suggest that you list the rights you are offering in the top right-hand corner of the first page (something like First North American Serial Rights, or Reprint Rights, or whatever). This is really unnecessary, since your cover letter will indicate if the story is new or has been previously published, and if previously published, where it originally appeared. As the editor of four anthologies of both new and reprint material, I've yet to see a professional writer list rights on his or her manuscript. Listing rights seems to me to be a flag to an editor that the writer is still a neophyte.

Paper quality

It would seem to be a matter of common sense other than something that had to be stated, but you should use a decent quality bond paper (20 lbs. bond is the norm) in sheets measuring 8.5" X 11". And of course, it should be white. This last suggestion might make you laugh, but I've heard stories of manuscripts printed in orange ink on yellow paper, and even one about a writer who inserted the carbon the wrong way in his typewriter and had the text come out reversed. Instead of re-typing the story, he asked the editor to hold the manuscript up to a mirror to read it.

There's nothing so obvious that it can go unsaid.

Print quality

Years ago, when computers first became a writer's tool, many guidelines specified no dot-matrix printouts, because the early printers were difficult to read. These days most printers do a great job, so there's no longer a need to stipulate what type of printout is preferred. If you're still using a dot-matrix printer, just make sure that the ribbon is fresh and you've set it on "near-letter quality," and if you're using a bubble-jet or laser printer, don't let the ink or toner cartridge run too low before replacing it. A manuscript that's difficult to read will make an editor less inclined to buy it.

It used to be common practice to include a large self-addressed, stamped envelope (SASE) with your submission so the entire manuscript could be returned to you, allowing you to send it out again to the next market. These days, with high-tech printers and copiers, it's easier (and cheaper) just to include a letter-sized SASE so the editor can send you a rejection letter (along with the first page of your manuscript so you know what's been rejected) or a contract. Since the whole point of using proper manuscript format is to give an editor an easily readable, professional-looking manuscript, it's best to produce a new manuscript each time you want to make a submission.

Staples and paper clips

It's a definite no-no to staple your story together at the top left-hand corner, much as it would make sense to do so. Editors like to be able to shuffle pages, and when a story is read, the finished page is usually slipped to the back of the sheaf. Stapling a corner prevents this and makes the type at the corners of the manuscript more difficult to read.

Paper clips are a good alternative, but some editors — the late fantasist Marion Zimmer Bradley comes to mind — have stated in their guidelines that they want nothing at all binding manuscript pages together.

Contest format

Sometimes magazines ask that you submit your story in contest or competition format. That means that all the information about who you are and how you can be contacted is typed on the first page of the manuscript along with the title of the story. Your story begins on page two, *with* the title of your story but *without* your name on it, while each of the page headers on the following pages consist of just the story title and a page number. This format allows "blind judging": the judges in the contest never see the contestants' names, and so won't be swayed by a writer's name or past works and will judge each story on its own merits.

Until just a few years ago, the Canadian magazine of speculative fiction, *On Spec*, required submissions to be in contest format. Now all that is required is proper manuscript format.

Manuscript Format for Novels

Manuscript format for novels doesn't differ all that much from the format used for short stories, but there are a couple of specifics you should keep in mind.

Title page

The main difference between manuscript formats for short stories and novels is that your novel will begin with a title page that will have your name and address in the top left-hand corner, as well as the name and contact information of your agent, if you happen to have one.

The word count (this time a number over 40,000) appears in the top right-hand corner. In the middle of the page is the novel's title, perhaps a line placing the novel in a particular genre, and your name or pseudonym, should you choose to use one. The rest of the manuscript follows the rules outlined previously in this chapter.

Chapter openers

Novels are broken into chapters, so you'll have to identify the start of each chapter. Start chapters on a new page, with the chapter heading (Chapter One; ONE; 1) on a line by itself about halfway down the page. As mentioned before, this will give an editor space to make notes about specific chapters while reading through the novel.

11
Sending off your manuscript

Now that you've finished your horror story, let it simmer a while, done revisions, and tightened it up like a clock spring, you can start *thinking* about sending it to a magazine editor. But before you go charging off to the mailbox, there are still a few things you need to do before your story is truly ready to land on an editor's desk.

Cover Letters

A cover letter introduces you to an editor, and perhaps tells him or her a bit about your story. But writing a cover letter for your story can be awkward, especially for a new writer. How much do you include, and what do you leave out?

Well, here's what you include:

- If you've ever sold a piece of your writing, mention that. Even if it's just a few articles to the local newspaper, it still tells the editor that you have some writing ability.

- If your story is set in an interesting place, like the sewers beneath the city of Toronto, and you have some particular knowledge about the setting, mention that. Say, "The story is set in

151

the sewers beneath Toronto, with which I'm quite familiar, having been a City sewer worker the past nine years." This lets the editor know that anything incredible or peculiar about the setting is probably based on fact.

- If you have a particular knowledge about the subject matter of your story, mention that. If you've written a ghost story and your hobby is searching for paranormal activity, then that just might pique the editor's interest.

- If a respected author or editor had suggested that you send the story to a particular magazine, you might want to mention that, since many authors or editors know what is appropriate for other magazines. An editor may look at a manuscript differently knowing that a peer thinks it might work in his or her magazine.

- If you've submitted to the magazine before, make mention of it. Editors admire perseverance. Even if an editor doesn't remember your last submission, he or she might be impressed that you've sent in another story.

- If you've met the editor at a lecture, convention, or party, you can mention that too. Again, though the editor might not recall meeting you (they are usually introduced to many young writers wherever they go), it will help you to make a connection, however tentative, with the editor.

Of course, none of this will get your story accepted if it isn't appropriate for the magazine you've sent it to, but dealing professionally with an editor could help you sell your 4th, 5th, or 20th submission, so you might as well start the ball rolling now.

And just as there's a list of things you should include in a cover letter, there are also things that you should leave out.

Here's a list of what not to include:

- Don't tell the editor what the story is about. If the editor is sharp, and most usually are, he or she will want to personally find this out.

- Don't tell the editor that the story is good, or that your wife/husband/mother/brother really, really liked it. The only opinion that counts is the editor's, and he or she will be the one to decide if the story is good or not.

- Don't mention anything about how hard you worked on the story or how much time you've spent writing it. It doesn't concern an editor that he or she rejects a story that someone took a year to write, or accepts a story that someone dashed off in a few hours. The only thing that matters is the quality of the work.

SASEs

SASE stands for self-addressed stamped envelope. If you want to get a response to your manuscript submission, make certain you include an SASE with your manuscript. In fact, if you want a response to any sort of query — for example, for writers' guidelines, or to find out if a magazine accepts reprints — an SASE is mandatory. The reality is that magazines receive up to 1,000 manuscripts per month, and if they had to pay for return postage on all of them, and on the various queries that come in from authors, there would be little money with which to pay contributors and print the magazine.

SASEs are also a good idea if you are writing to an author to ask some question, request an autograph, or would just like to get a response for whatever reason.

And here's another obvious thing, but it needs to be mentioned. If you live in Canada and are submitting a story to the United States, your SASE must have American stamps on it. The same is true for an American writer submitting to a Canadian market. When I edited the anthology Northern Horror, about 30 percent of the submissions from American writers had American stamps on them. One writer didn't bother to include any postage at all, only a self-addressed envelope (SAE). If you cannot get stamps for a specific country, buy an International Reply Coupon (IRC) from the post office (in any country around the world) and include that with your SAE. The editor will then exchange the coupon for postage, so he can provide you with a response. IRCs are more expensive than stamps, but they do the same job. A better alternative is to stock up on stamps whenever you visit Canada or the US, or have a friend do it for you. I myself have a small sewing box that has numerous compartments for threads, and in each compartment I keep an assortment of US, Canadian, and British stamps, as well as one or two IRCs.

Simultaneous Submissions

When you send off your story, choose the publication wisely, because you'll be sending it to one publication at a time and it might be a long time before you'll hear word on whether it's been accepted or rejected.

When I first began submitting my stories for publication, three months was a long time to wait for a response. After three months I would send a polite follow-up letter as a reminder to the editor about how long he or she had to look at the story, and shortly after that I'd get my story back.

Today it seems that three months is not much time to wait at all, and response times of eight or ten months, or even more than a year, are not unheard of. As a result, simultaneous submissions — submission of the same story to more than one magazine at the same time — have become more accepted among editors. So instead of your story going to one magazine for three to six months, and then to another for a similarly long time, it goes out to ten magazines at once and has a chance of selling more quickly than it might otherwise.

Sounds great, but not all magazines are willing to look at simultaneous submissions. Their reason is this: Why should an editor spend time considering a manuscript when, by the time he or she decides to buy it, it might already have been taken by another magazine? However, some editors don't mind that a story has been sent to more than one market, as long as you mention in your cover letter that you are simultaneously submitting the story elsewhere.

If in doubt, check the publication's guidelines or query the editor first. Nothing will irritate an editor more than accepting a story, only to be told by the author that it has already been accepted somewhere else.

Rolling Submissions

Because of the long waiting periods encountered by writers in recent years, many have opted for a strategy called a rolling submission.

Here's how it works: When you submit your story, you mention in your cover letter that the editor has an exclusive look at the story for a period of three months. If you haven't received a response in three months, you will assume the editor is not interested in the manuscript, and you will then send it to another publication. And so on, and so on...

This seems to be a happy medium between making single and simultaneous submissions. It gives the editor a fair amount of time to consider the manuscript, but it doesn't tie up a writer's work for an unreasonable period.

E-mail Submissions

Some magazines accept e-mail submissions; in fact, some even prefer them. Obviously, electronic magazines lead the way in terms of e-mail submissions, but print magazines are slowly catching up. If you know the e-mail address of a magazine but are unsure if they accept submissions through that account, send a query or check the magazine's guidelines for a mention of electronic submissions. Many editors do all of their correspondence via e-mail but prefer that submissions be made through snail mail.

If you're going to submit a story by e-mail, make sure it is in a plain text like ASCII or inside the body of your e-mail letter. While you can send attached files in WordPerfect and MS Word over the Internet, you can never be sure if your file can be read at the other end. For that reason you should send the text as simply as possible, and then in a preferred format after an editor requests it.

12
Getting a Response

Once you submit a manuscript to a magazine, publisher, or agent, the best thing you can do is forget all about it and start working on your next novel or story. Many new writers agonize over their first few stories, counting the days and watching their mailboxes, thinking that every day that passes without a response means their manuscripts are being seriously considered. The truth is, your manuscript is probably sitting in a pile with a hundred others and will stay there for weeks, or months, until an editor has a chance to read it.

In the case of novels, it can take up to two years to get a response, even though the decision on the book might take only a few minutes to make. And though I can't verify it as being true or just a sort of urban legend, I have heard of one novel manuscript being at a publisher for years because it was under a leg of an editor's desk to keep it level. That might be a little farfetched, but if you realize it as a possibility, you'll probably be more patient when awaiting a response.

Form Rejections

When you finally do get a response, it will likely be a form rejection letter. Typical language for such a letter would be something like this one from *Alfred Hitchcock's Mystery Magazine*:

Thank you very much for the opportunity to read your manuscript. Unfortunately, it does not meet our needs at this time.

Your story has been read by one or more members of our staff, but we regret that the press of time and the number of manuscripts we receive prohibit us from making a personal reply or giving criticism.

We do wish you the best of luck in finding a publisher for your story elsewhere.

The Editors

Not all that encouraging, but it is honest. The story may have been read by more than one editor, and it might have been close to being accepted, but the sheer volume of manuscripts — *Hitchcock's* and *Ellery Queen*, which have been known to publish horror stories on occasion, receive roughly 1,000 manuscripts per month — prevents them from answering each submission individually.

Other form rejections, including the ones used by many of the smaller horror magazines, are of an entirely different nature. In addition to the standard line about the editor considering your story and deciding that "It's not quite right for us," there is another section to the letter with a list of comments the editor can check off in response to your story.

For example, the magazine *Deathrealm* used to send out a rejection slip with preprinted comments such as —

✓ *Horrible (in the best sense of the word), but not for us.*

✓ *Well-written; nice, but the story didn't work for us.*

✓ *Very/Somewhat predictable; better try a new route.*

But it also has comments like —

✓ *In need of polishing or improved prose.*

✓ *Populated by stupid characters. No thanks.*

✓ *In improper manuscript format — better fix quick!*

Finally, the *Deathrealm* rejection slip's last comment is one no one would want to get.

✓ *Devoid of any redeeming qualities — try plumbing.*

Pretty harsh, but not all that unique. The final comment on the old Borderlands Press form rejection letter reads:

✓ *Have you ever considered an alternative career? I hear hotel/motel management, frozen food packaging, and re-tailing women's foundation undergarments can all be very rewarding.*

Funny stuff, but not to be taken seriously. I've heard editors say that they include a comment like that so that the rejected author can say to himself or herself, "Well, at least they didn't check off *that* one!"

Personalized Rejections

Even some of the form rejection letters with preprinted comments have blank lines on them to allow an editor to make his or her own comment or two on the manuscript. This could be anything from a simple "Hi!" to a few comments on the manuscript, like this one I received from Jamie Meyers, editor of the now defunct small-press horror magazine *Doppleganger*.

Dear Edo,

Great to hear from you again. "Lip-O-Suction" is well done, but it just doesn't throw me one way or the other. It's an original idea, though, and pretty gross to boot. Good luck marketing it. And try again soon!

J.M.

Encouraging? Sure was at the time, but also frustrating. "Lip-O-Suction" is about a fat-sucking vampire who uses his talents to operate a weight-loss clinic. At the time it was as original a story as I could come up with, but it still didn't sell to this editor, to whom I'd been sending stories on a regular basis.

What you must always remember is that an editor's opinion is the opinion of only one person. Another editor might think the story great and be thrilled to publish it. "Lip-O-Suction" was eventually published in the small-press magazine, *The Vampire's Crypt,* then reprinted in my short story collection, *Death Drives a Semi.*

But while getting personalized rejection letters may mean you've reached a certain level in your development as a writer, it doesn't mean that those letters will all be complimentary.

The worst rejection I ever received was a completely personal letter from *Weird Tales* editor George Scithers:

> *Dear Edo:*
>
> *Thanks for showing us "That Will Be All." Alas; this is more a Revelation of the Formalities of the Hereafter than a complete story about them — basically, these pieces of paper that have been typed on leave the reader with that fatal question, "Is that all?"*
>
> *Sincerely,*
>
> *George H. Scithers*

The worst part of the rejection was that he didn't even call my story a *story.* Instead, he referred to it as "these pieces of paper that have been typed on." This happened in 1988 and could have stopped my writing career in its tracks. But instead of crying in my beer, I took the comments about the story to heart, added a new ending to it, and eventually placed it in *Haunts* magazine. In a final triumph of writerly determination, the magazine actually chose to place my name on the cover of the issue, as in "New Works by."

Which brings me to a crucial point about horror writers and their careers.

Don't Give Up — Be Determined

Here's a list and a rule to remember:

1. Talent.
2. Luck.
3. Persistence.

Any two of these three qualities is required to become a successful writer.

You can have talent and be lucky.

You can have talent and persist.

You can persist and get lucky.

Notice that one of the alternatives does not even require talent. Of course, if you want to see your work published, you must have some ability to string words together, but you don't have to have a blazing talent. However, if you don't have talent, then you must have persistence; more than that, you must have a dogged determination to succeed.

Why? Because as you write and submit your stories, there will be many people along the way who will tell you your work is not good enough. And some won't be too polite about it either.

Or say that you do succeed and sell a novel. Say you spent two years working on the book, then took another couple of years to sell it. But when you sell it, it's for only a few thousand dollars (the basic first-novel advance will run somewhere between $1,500 to $5,000), not the tens or hundreds of thousands you envisioned. Then the novel is published with a cover that embarrasses you, with a small print run that barely puts one book in each major book store. The publisher does nothing to promote the book, sales are dismal, and some of the reviews seem to take glee in trashing your creation. You've invested some four years of your life in return for little money and little satisfaction, and in the end you wonder why on Earth you wanted to do this in the first place.

Persistence and determination are an integral part of a writer's career. If you don't believe me, perhaps you might believe Stephen King. When I was starting out, I enlarged this quotation from *Bare Bones,* a book of Stephen King interviews, and taped it onto the wall just above my monitor. Whenever I got depressed or didn't feel like working, I read the quote to remind myself that everyone struggles at some point in his or her career.

> In a way, with those early (unpublished) novels, I felt like a guy who was plugging quarters in the machine with the big jackpot. And yanking it down. And at first they were coming up all wrong. Then with the book before Carrie, felt I got two bars and a lemon; then with Carrie, bars across the board — and the money poured out. But the thing is, I was never convinced I was going to run out of quarters to plug into the machine. My feeling was, I could stand there forever until it hit. There was never

That's the trick to being a writer; every time you get rejected you do a handspring up and land on your feet, amazing your opponent.

— RICK HAUTALA

really any doubt in my mind. A couple of times I felt I was pursuing a fool's dream, but those moments were rare.

Network with Others in the Field

If you're having trouble selling your horror stories, you're not alone. There are hundreds of aspiring writers going through the exact same thing you are. What's worse, each of them is thinking, just as you are, that he or she is the only one who is struggling. Which, of course, just isn't true.

There are plenty of writers out there, and practically every one of them had to struggle at some point in their careers. It does a body good to meet other writers and talk about being rejected and how to make your stories better.

A writers' organization like the Horror Writers Association can be helpful to those getting into the field. As a member, you can connect with others who are in the same position as you are and you can exchange thoughts, words of encouragement, and market information with each other via e-mail or through good-old-fashioned snail mail.

But what if you're not online, or you'd rather meet people in the flesh? Every small city or town has a writing group or workshop in which writers get together and talk shop. A library is a good place to start looking for a group or directories of clubs and associations put out by the city.

You could also attend an author's reading at a local bookstore and ask questions. Most authors are only too happy to share stories of their early efforts to get published, and some might be able to steer you in the direction of a local writers' group or connect you with another struggling author.

If All Else Fails, Start Your Own Small Magazine

Some new writers in the horror field connect with other new writers by starting up a magazine. The idea is not so new; even Stephen King published his own stories, along with stories by childhood friend Chris Chesley, in an 18-page publication called *People, Places and Things*, back in 1963.

Say the material you're writing doesn't fit the requirements of most of the genre magazines being published today, but you're sure that your work is good enough to be in print. If you start your own small magazine, you can slip one of your stories into its pages, and you'll be in regular contact with other writers and editors, who will invariably submit to your magazine. Even if you resist the temptation to publish your own fiction in your magazine (don't forget there's still plenty of room for you to write reviews, editorials, and nonfiction), you'll be networking with other writers and editors, and this will make you known to them.

Obviously, this is only a way to get your horror-writing career *started*, not a way to *build* yourself a career. Sales to your own magazine won't impress many people, and certainly not the editors of professional magazines. If and when you start selling to other publications on a semi-regular basis, it might be time to pass the magazine's operation on to someone else, or to close it down altogether so that you can concentrate on writing and selling horror fiction, rather than publishing it.

13
the horror marketplace

Short Fiction

Small-press magazines

Small-press magazines are usually one-person operations in which the editor is everything from publisher to chief cook and bottle washer. The publications are not very elaborate and are often printed up on someone's office photocopier, then stapled together in someone else's living room. Obviously, the production values of these magazines (often called zines) can be lacking, although they can sometimes have excellent content. Payment is usually in copies of the magazine in which your work appears.

On the up side, small-press magazines don't get many submissions from established writers, so they are open to new writers, even first-timers. But since many small-press magazines are produced by a single person, submitters can expect long response times and even longer times between a story's acceptance and its eventual appearance in print. And because the magazine's health depends on the health — physical, emotional, and financial — of the person running it, oftentimes a magazine will fold before your story has had a chance to be published.

My all-time rejection leader, "But Somebody's Got to Do It," (rejected 24 times before seeing print in my collection, *Death Drives a Semi*) was accepted for publication three times along the way by magazines that didn't live long enough to publish the story. It has since been reprinted.

Semi-professional magazines

Semi-professional magazines usually have some decent production values and pay a modest amount for stories. Payment can range from one-quarter cent per word (a token payment, really) to two cents per word (a slightly higher token payment). These magazines are usually run by two or more people (usually volunteers) who put out the magazine because they enjoy it. They do their best to keep up a regular publication schedule and keep to it for a few years before running out of money, interest, or time.

As the production quality of semi-professional magazines is a big step up from the small press, so too is the quality of the fiction inside. They might not pay as much as the bigger publications, but semi-pro magazines are able to take greater risks with what they publish. As a result, many excellent stories find their way into the semi-pro press.

Canada's *On Spec* is a semi-professional magazine paying two to three Canadian cents per word for fiction. It's been regularly published as a quarterly, perfect-bound digest for more than ten years and has a circulation that constantly flirts with the number 1,000. In 1997, it published "Rat Food," which I co-authored with David Nickle, and which won the Horror Writers Association's Bram Stoker Award for superior achievement in a short story the following year.

Professional magazines

What constitutes a professional magazine? Both the Science Fiction and Fantasy Writers of America and the Horror Writers Association have their own guidelines, but, except for a few slight variations, these are pretty much the same.

In simple terms, a professional magazine is one that publishes on a regular basis (three or four issues a year); has a minimum circulation of a few thousand (each organization requires a different minimum number); and must pay at least three cents US per word.

The minimum professional payment rate is just that, a minimum. Most top genre magazines like *Cemetery Dance, Weird Tales,* and the *Magazine of Fantasy and Science Fiction* pay upward of five cents per word. A better pay rate can usually be had when selling a horror story outside the genre. Magazines like *Playboy* and *Penthouse* pay up to $5,000 per story, but don't publish all that many stories in a year and only a few by new or unknown writers.

On the down side, it is obviously much harder to sell a story to a professional magazine than it is to sell to a small-press one. However, once you've sold a story to a pro market, you can be pretty sure that the story will be published, and the credential is one that will put you in good stead with other magazine and book editors in the field.

Anthologies

Anthologies are collections of short stories by many different authors. The stories usually revolve around a certain theme or idea. For example, the *Hot Blood* series were anthologies of erotic horror stories, and the *Northern Frights* series contained horror tales by Canadian writers and stories by American writers that were set in Canada.

It can be hard for new writers to crack an anthology lineup, as not all anthology editors allow open submissions. The slush pile (the pile of stories yet to be read) often contains work of poor quality or that doesn't pertain to the anthology's particular theme; reading through it can be a waste of an editor's time. Many editors avoid the slush pile altogether by inviting submissions only from a limited number of writers whose work they admire or whom they would like to have contribute to their anthology. Still other editors pick and choose their contributors and commission writers who they know will provide a good story for their anthology. The editor is pretty much bound to take what the writer produces, so anthology editors commission stories only from writers whose work they know well or who have a good number of quality stories to their credit.

But just because many anthologies are closed to new writers doesn't mean new writers can't submit to them. All it takes is a professional attitude.

When I read the first *Shock Rock* anthology, edited by Jeff Gelb, I sent him a letter telling him how much I enjoyed the book and asking that if he did another, could I please submit a story to it? He never answered me, but when I heard that he was indeed editing another volume, I sent another letter reminding him of my previous letter and

A Few Words With...

Don Hutchison

on eδιτιng horror anthologies

EDO VAN BELKOM: What was the most difficult part about putting together the *Northern Frights* anthologies?

DON HUTCHISON: Our series was conceived as a market for original stories of quality by writers of any stripe, whether big names or talented unknowns. The problem with an open market is that it prompts a monstrous quantity of unsolicited material. When I first started reading for the book I greeted each new story with excitement and enthusiasm. But you soon begin to realize that most submissions will not be good enough for publication and not bad enough to be truly entertaining. And then there's the unenviable task of writing rejection letters to all those anxious hopefuls. You try to put yourself in their place and be as sympathetic and as helpful as time permits. It's a sifting process that eventually pays off, but handing out rejections, sympathetic or otherwise, is not a pleasant task.

EDO VAN BELKOM: What would you say was lacking most in the majority of stories you rejected?

DON HUTCHISON: A simple one-word answer would be, "Originality." The author's most jaded critic is surely his first — the long-suffering editor or slush-pile reader who has struggled through numerous versions of plots and situations all too familiar to anyone conversant with the genre. If you don't have something new to say and perhaps a new way of saying it, why bother at all? But originality alone is not enough. The horror field is not enriched by tales of madness and mayhem devoid of meaningful context — you can get those at your local video store and on the six o'clock news. I feel that too many would-be horror authors enter the field with little knowledge or appreciation of its history.

The classic horror story is not something cheap and exploitative invented by Hollywood, nor is it a bastard son of pulp fiction. While a science fiction story may get by on a particularly novel idea and a mystery tale on a clever plot, effective horror fiction must build up suspense and atmosphere with a subtle accretion of style, characterization, balance, and narrative energy, all relating in some manner to the human experience. At its best, the horror story is literature — *real* literature — with a long and honorable history. I feel that writers steeped in that tradition have the best chance to come up with new and exciting variations.

EDO VAN BELKOM: As an editor, what advice could you give to aspiring horror writers who would like to submit to anthologies?

DON HUTCHISON: First of all, get to know the market you submit to. One anthology is not the same as another — at least it shouldn't be. Nor is the taste of one editor exactly the same as another. As I frequently tell authors of rejected stories, horror, like humor, is subjective. What one person finds funny may leave another cold. And what one person finds frightening may appear merely silly to another. So only by reading what an editor publishes can you judge what rings his or her bell. Speaking personally, I have received numerous submissions that simply do not fit our stated requirements. Many of these submissions have requested sample copies of our *Northern Frights* "magazine," revealing their ignorance of what the hell it is we are actually publishing.

It may seem obvious, but submit only one story at a time. An envelope wadded with half-a-dozen stories smells of previous rejections — as does unclean copy bearing coffee rings and smudges. Keep cover letters brief and to the point. Do not compose chummy notes to editors you do not know personally. They are not interested in your private life or the fact that your story is based on something that actually happened to your Aunt Agatha. A mention of previous sales to professional markets will get you an interested read, but lists of appearances in obscure "semi-pro" magazines may not.

> Most important, submit only your very best work. If the story doesn't quite work for you, it probably won't work for others either. Put it away but don't give up on it if it has merit. Some of the best stories we have published have been those that gave their authors initial problems — right up until the bright day when a different slant or a fresh, inspired ending transmuted a "difficult" story into something new and wonderful.
>
> ---
>
> *Don Hutchison is the creator and editor of the award-winning* Northern Frights *anthology series as well as the author of the non-fiction book,* The Great Pulp Heroes.

asked him again if I could submit a story. This time he answered, sending the guidelines not only for *Shock Rock 2,* but also for two other anthologies he was working on at the time: *Fear Itself* and *Hot Blood 4.* Never one to let an opportunity like this to go to waste, I submitted — and sold — stories to all three anthologies.

Horror on the Web

The Internet represents a new frontier for horror fiction. There are dozens, if not hundreds, of Web sites that publish horror fiction, both from established pros and new writers alike. Web zines are the fastest-growing marketplace for horror fiction, and some interesting marketing is currently happening on the Internet.

The reason for this?

No overhead.

When someone produces a print magazine, there are costs involved (printing, postage, etc.) — the last of which, it seems, is paying the authors for their work. Not so on the Web. Anyone can hang a shingle on his or her own Web page proclaiming it to be an online magazine, without having to shell out a dime past the cost of a computer and Web server.

As a result, there is currently a proliferation of horror e-zines on the Web, and some, like *Gothic.Net,* pay professional word rates for fiction. Others, such as *Eternity Online,* pay semi-professional rates. However, these magazines represent the top of the Web, so to speak. As you travel further down the line you'll find that most Web zines pay one cent a word or nothing at all.

Which raises a couple of questions.

If a Web zine has little or no overhead but doesn't pay its contributors anything, what impetus drives the editor to be critical about the quality of the work he publishes? And if a Web zine pays nothing, and very few people will be reading the stories posted on it, what might the quality of the fiction be?

The World Wide Web is an expanding market for horror fiction and, like the small press, is a good place to get started but not to forge a career. Of course, this sort of talk is aimed at those who want to write horror stories and have them published professionally. If, however, you're only interested in writing horror for fun and for the entertainment of your friends and family, the Web is a place that's made to order.

For the professional horror writer, the Internet provides a unique marketing opportunity that never before existed in the genre. For example, many authors have their own Web sites on which they feature news about themselves and their work, and even some of their own fiction. Another inventive use of the Internet was made by Douglas Clegg, author of such novels as *Goat Dance* and *The Children's Hour,* who published an entire novel, *Naomi,* via the Internet in 1999, sending a chapter a week free to anyone who provided him with an e-mail address. Although he earned nothing by sending the story out, he did garner some valuable publicity, including articles in *Publisher's Weekly* and other industry and genre publications. The entire novel is currently available at <www.douglasclegg.com>.

Here's a list of Web sites that are full of items of interest to the horror writer or reader, including book reviews, author profiles, news, and links to other sites, especially author sites:

www.darkecho.com	www.horrorOnline.com
www.darkmuse.com	www.darktales.com
www.frightnet.com	www.horrornet.com
www.gothic.net	www.drcasey.com

A Few Words With...

Douglas Clegg

on horror on the web

EDO VAN BELKOM: You've done something quite unique with your novel *Naomi*, sending it out free in weekly installments via e-mail. What was the reason for doing the novel that way?

DOUGLAS CLEGG: Writing is about communicating with readers as much as it is finding the core of the imagination. You need both. The Web is a potentially explosive communication tool. So there's that. Then, I had *The Nightmare Chronicles* and *You Come When I Call You* coming out in what Web people call dead-trees (paper) form, and my online publicist and her assistant pretty much suggested I do some kind of giveaway online at some point. "Well," I thought, "why not a novel?" I wasn't sure how to do this, and the more I looked into it, the more I realized that in fact it hadn't quite been done the way I intended to do it, so I figured, "Good. I'll try something a little bit different." Other writers on the Web — from Brian Hopkins to David Niall Wilson — and many others outside the horror genre — had been giving away fiction on the Web, but coming from a solid mass-market background, I really felt I had more to risk (in terms of selling the novel for a sum of money and then later making royalties) than many of the other projects. I knew *Naomi* could go to a mass-market house and come out, and that would be nice (and it still may, later on down the road). But I wanted to take the risk, since I think the Web has a seed of the future for writers, and I figured I might as well jump in as well as anyone.

I also always feel guilty for ever allowing people to pay to read my fiction. I'm a bit of a "take it, it's free" kind of guy, which I'm sure is one of the most unprofessional things a writer can admit. I like publishers to pay me, but I think fiction should be free for readers.... Since this makes no sense, I figured I'd just give one book to readers in electronic form as a kind of gift. *Naomi* was a novel I'd been trying to figure out for several years, and since it was time to write it, I figured, "Well, this is next up, and now I'll do something special with it." I never expected *BusinessWeek, Publisher's Weekly,* and various regional and college newspapers to pick up the story, as well as the Associated Press. I figured it was just my little novel that I hoped readers would enjoy.

Luckily, a publisher — Leisure — actually ended up sponsoring *Naomi,* which meant cash in my pocket. In turn, I used some of it for paying for ads on Web zines that traditionally might not have an influx of outside cash, as well as for paying someone for maintaining all the *Naomi* stuff.

EDO VAN BELKOM: Besides *Naomi,* have you published any other horror fiction on the Web, or do you even submit to Web zines?

DOUGLAS CLEGG: I don't submit to Web zines, at least not in a business sense. I've had online fiction at <www.horrornet.com/clegg.htm>, my alter ego Web presence that Matt Schwartz set up; and then, when "I Am Infinite; I Contain Multitudes" was nominated for a Stoker, Wayne Edwards was nice enough to set that up online for readers for a little while. I've sometimes offered a reprint of a story to a Web zine. But no, I don't pursue the Web zines as a rule. Again, I really like to get paid by publishers, and Web zines often don't have the budgets. When they do, I'll probably start selling stories to them; in the meantime, I'll just keep selling short stories offline. But I do think that Web zines are great proving grounds for writers. Unfortunately, I think they're often used as vanity presses with no thought to a fictive imagination or even to readers.

EDO VAN BELKOM: What role do you think the World Wide Web will play in the future in terms of horror-fiction publishing?

DOUGLAS CLEGG: I think it will be an adjunct to all mass-market publishing. Paper prices have been skyrocketing, and the expenses of the paperbound industry have gone up. As a result, profits for books will go down. And yet here we have a technology that involves no paper. I use a Rocket e-book for reading various novels and nonfiction books, and it's terrific. Now, I still like to pick up a hardback or paperback to read, too. But it's just an alternative method of reading that is potentially more economically and ecologically sound (although I still feel that electricity has its own eco-evil built into it).

I think Web zines will flourish for a long time to come because they're a terrific place for aspiring writers to work and get feedback — a nice way to pay dues and fall on your face, which I think we all need to do to get to the point of understanding the craft of fiction writing. Electronic publishing is part of the future, so we may as well face it. Someday, I think there will be networks, just like in television and radio, and all of this will be more corporate and regulated. Right now, the Web is the Wild West, and anyone can stake his or her claim. That's exciting. It's also totally crazy, which is wonderful, too.

―――――――――――

Douglas Clegg is the author of nine novels, including Goat Dance, The Children's Hour, The Halloween Man, *and* You Come When I Call You. *His first collection of short stories,* The Nightmare Chronicles, *was published in the fall of 1999.*

He can be reached at <DougClegg@aol.com>, or through his Web site at <www.douglasclegg.com>.

Book-Length Horror

Novels

The market for horror novels has seen better days.

Horror had always been a strong-selling type of fiction, but it never had its own section in the bookstore until the late 1970s, when Stephen King became a huge success and every other publisher scrambled to find its own master of the macabre. As a result, the 1980s were a boom time for horror, with each major publishing house (Tor, Bantam, Avon,

Warner, Ballantine, Zebra, Leisure, Berkeley, NAL, and Pocket) carrying a line of horror novels that featured 2 to 4 new paperbacks each month. That worked out to between 24 and 48 horror novels per year for each house and a total of perhaps more than 500 new horror titles published each year.

With that many horror novels being published, you might wonder as to the general quality of the books. Sadly, most were not very good, and as a result the horror market boom of the 1980s went bust by the start of the 1990s. Many novelists who had thought they'd established themselves as horror writers and were publishing a new novel every year or so (in some cases every six months) suddenly found themselves without publishers.

Despite the crash of the horror market, horror novels were still published through the 1990s, but they no longer sported the word HORROR on their spines, and book covers no longer sported possessed dolls, grinning skeletons, or demonic children. The mediocre titles that had been able to find a publisher in a market that was hungry for horror, any horror, were dropped. Excellent horror novels, like Robert McCammon's *Boy's Life*, Peter Straub's *The Throat*, and Joyce Carol Oates's *Zombie*, were all published to great acclaim in the 1990s. And while the mainstream might not have recognized each one as a horror novel, the Horror Writers Association had no trouble identifying the works as horror and recognized each with a Bram Stoker Award for superior achievement in the novel form.

New writers were also able to get a foothold in the horror field in the lean early 1990s. Kathe Koja, now considered a top mainstream writer, broke into the horror field in 1991 with her first novel, *The Cipher*, and other top writers who grew to prominence in the 1990s include Jay R. Bonansinga, Michael Slade, and Matthew J. Costello.

The bottom line is that there will always be a market for good horror, but there is no better time than now for an aspiring horror writer to possess the qualities of persistence and patience, in addition to talent.

Media tie-ins

Media tie-ins are novels set in some sort of media universe, such as the *X-Files* television series, the *X-men* comic-book series, or the *Ravenloft* role-play game. Since most often these books need to be written quickly, they are usually assigned to a professional writer with a proven track record. In the horror genre, Charles L. Grant is one writer who often does this sort of book, either under his own name or a pseudonym. However, that doesn't mean that new writers can't break into the horror-book market by this means. Many comic-book writers, role-play game designers, even hard-core fans got their start writing media tie-in novels.

My first novel, *Wyrm Wolf*, was based on the White Wolf Game Studio role-play game *Werewolf: The Apocalypse*. I had written several short stories for the company, and when I heard they had a contract with HarperPrism for six novels based on their games, I contacted White Wolf and suggested to them that I do one of the novels. They agreed, and I ended up doing two novels for them, *Wyrm Wolf* and *Mister Magick*.

Novelizations

Unlike media tie-ins, which are original stories set in a media universe, novelizations are novels based on movie, television, or CD-ROM scripts. Just as the word suggests, a writer takes the script and fills it out with characterization, description, and backstory — motivation, history, and other events not specifically mentioned in the script — thereby turning it into a novel.

But while media tie-ins can occasionally be open to new writers, novelizations almost always go to experienced writers who can do the work quickly (usually in a couple of months) or to a writer (not necessarily a novelist) who is close to the television or movie project and can be given the job of novelizing his or her own script. However, there are always exceptions to the rule. David J. Schow, now a successful Hollywood writer with many screen and television credits to his name, actually started out writing *Miami Vice* novelizations under the name Stephen Grave.

Some of the best horror writers doing novelizations include Dennis Etchison *(The Fog)*; Matthew J. Costello *(Child's Play 2, Child's Play 3)*; Ray Garton *(Warlock, Invaders from Mars)* and Alan Dean Foster *(Alien, The Thing)*.

Markets outside the Horror Genre

Publishers don't have publishing programs devoted exclusively to the horror genre, but many mainstream houses are publishing horror under the guise of dark suspense, romance, or mystery.

As an example of how new writers can break in with novels published outside of the horror genre, I give you the final ballot for the 1995 Bram Stoker Award in the first-novel category. Discarding my own *Wyrm Wolf,* a novel based on a role-play game, each of the four other first-novel finalists were published by either a small press or by a large publisher, not as a horror novel, but as a mainstream title. *Diary of a Vampire,* by Gary Bowen, was published by erotica publisher Masquerade Books. *The Between,* by Tananarive Due, was published by Harper Collins. *Madeline's Ghost,* by Robert Girardi, was published by Delacorte Press. And *The Safety of Unknown Cities,* was published by Silver Salamander Press. And so the list reads small specialty house, mainstream publisher, mainstream publisher, small press. None of the books on the ballot were published by a major house as a "horror" novel.

There are many ways to get your novel published. You just have to be creative and persistent in finding the one that's right for you.

Robert Heinlein's Five Rules of Writing

1. You must write.

2. You must finish what you start.

3. You must refrain from rewriting, except to editorial order.*

4. You must put it on the market.

5. You must keep it on the market until it is sold.

(*Rule number three assumes that the story is absolutely as good as you can possibly make it, and therefore requires no further revision.)

Book Publishers

Major publishers

Stephen King, Anne Rice, Dean Koontz, John Saul, and Clive Barker will always have markets for their novels. Having a marketable name is like gold. Just think: V.C. Andrews has been dead for many years now, but books are still being published under her name even though they are being written by Andrew Neiderman, a fine horror writer in his own right.

But in horror, as in science fiction, the publisher's midlist (where a writer could make a living writing one or two moderately successful paperback originals each year) has virtually disappeared, leaving publishers with big-name writers like the ones mentioned above. However, every once in a while a new name emerges from the lists of the big publishing houses. Tananarive Due and Jay Bonansinga have each published several fine horror novels and their careers appear to be flourishing.

Types of Books

A *chapbook* consists of usually less than 100 pages and will contain a single novella or a collection of a few stories. Most often, chapbooks are saddle stapled (i.e., a staple in the middle, as in a magazine) but can also be perfect bound (i.e., with a stiff spine).

Mass-market paperbacks are also known as pocket books. "Mass market" is used to describe them because print runs usually begin with 20,000 or 30,000 copies and the book reaches the widest possible audience.

A *trade paperback* is the size of a hardcover book, but has a paper cover and is priced midway between a mass-market paperback and a hardcover. Although more prestigious a format for an author's work, print runs are usually low, starting at 1,000 copies; 5,000 is a respectable number at the upper end.

Hardcovers are the usual first printings of major books by the likes of Stephen King, Anne Rice, and Peter Straub. They are expensive, well made, and as much for collecting and cherishing as for reading.

Omnibus editions collect two or more books into one volume, such as Stephen King's *Bachman Books*, which combines all four early Bachman (King's pseudonym) novels into a single book.

Anthologies are collections of stories by multiple authors, as opposed to a single-author collection, which is — as the label might suggest — several stories by the same author.

Small presses

In recent years, with the major publishing houses not actively seeking horror titles, many smaller publishers have moved in to fill the gap. New publishers like Cemetery Dance Publications, The Design Image Group, Meisha Merlin, and Quarry Press have started their own successful horror lines. While the days of the midlist mass-market paperback horror novel with a print run of 30,000 to 40,000 copies are gone, there is still a readership for inexpensive trade paperbacks with modest print runs of 1,000 to 5,000 copies. Also, many publishers are able to turn a profit in exquisitely designed limited editions in runs of 100 to 1,000 copies. These smaller houses might well be the future home of some of the best horror fiction.

Print-on-demand

The technology exists to publish one book at a time in an inexpensive binding that looks every bit as good as a volume that was part of a 10,000-copy print run. Babbage Press in California, is one company that publishes such books. Pulpless.com is another, providing customers the options of downloading a book for about $3.50 US or buying a physical copy of the book for about $20.00 US. When you order a book, a single copy is printed, bound, and sent to you.

The advantage of such a system is that books can remain "in print" forever and publishers can offer their entire backlist without any worries about warehouse space or constantly updating catalogues. For a writer, the prospect of having a book remain in print is a dream come true. And for a reader, knowing that a book will always be available is a very comforting thought.

However, this system works best for backlist titles. Most readers still like to browse the bookstore rather than flip through a catalogue, and it will be a few years yet before bookstores have the ability to print books on site and this system enjoys widespread popularity.

Electronic books

As with print-on-demand books, the technology now exists for electronic books to be easily read, either on hand-held viewscreens or downloaded onto personal computers via the Internet.

This type of publishing requires the reader to have some special equipment in order to read the books, and so it's a publishing venue for the future. Some firms already offer books in this manner, but paying the author solely for the number of times a title is downloaded doesn't translate into a lucrative market for the writer. The number of titles available electronically is currently very small, though growing.

Where to Find Market Information

One of the questions I'm most frequently asked when I give talks to writing classes is, "Where do I send my story when I'm finished writing it?" Fortunately, the horror genre is blessed with many sources of market information that are invaluable to new writers looking to make a first sale. Here's a list of some of the best sources around:

Scavengers Newsletter

Scavengers Newsletter is a monthly newsletter that lists new markets in the horror, science fiction, and fantasy genres. In addition to new markets, it notes changes to editorial guidelines of existing magazines, lists contests, records magazine response times, and publishes nonfiction articles on writing.

For more information, write to —

Scavengers Newsletter
Janet Fox, Editor
519 Ellinwood
Osage City, KS
USA 66523-1329
E-mail: <foxscav1@jc.net>

The Gila Queen's Guide to Markets

Published by horror writer Kathryn Ptacek, *The Gila Queen's Guide to Markets* is an irregular (almost monthly) magazine devoted to all types of writing markets. As well as providing new listings and updates, each issue features a different genre: one month the spotlight will be on romance, another it will be on horror.

For more information, write to —

The Gila Queen's Guide to Markets
Katherine Ptacek, Editor
PO Box 97
Newton, NJ
USA 07860-0097
E-mail: <GilaQueen@aol.com>

Writer's Digest Magazine Fiction 50

Each June the staff at *Writer's Digest* puts together a list of the top 50 fiction markets in the United States. It is a great reference list, although not complete, as some of the absolute best fiction markets like *Playboy* and *The New Yorker* aren't included. However, each year 5 or 6 of the 50 markets listed publish horror.

For more information, write to —

Writer's Digest Magazine
1507 Dana Avenue
Cincinnati, OH
USA 45207
Phone toll free (for a subscription): 1-800-333-0133

Annual *Novel and Short Story Writer's Market*

Each year the staff at Writer's Digest Books put out a series of annually updated books providing market information about different writing fields. The best one for a fiction writer is the annual *Novel and Short Story Writer's Market*. This book lists hundreds of small and commercial magazines, literary journals, contests, agents, and book publishers. However, don't confuse this book with the annual *Writer's Market*, which tries to give a little bit of market information on all types of writing and doesn't give enough information on fiction markets.

For more information, write to —

Novel and Short Story Writer's Market
Writer's Digest Books
1507 Dana Avenue
Cincinnati, OH
USA 45207

Writers' Organizations and Groups

Writers' organizations usually have membership numbers in the hundreds or thousands (such as the Horror Writers Association and the Science Fiction and Fantasy Writers of America) and provide their members with regular market information through their newsletters or online publications.

Writers' groups (for instance, the Writers Circle of Durham or the Brampton Writers Workshop) are more local in nature, and almost every small town or county has one. The major difference is that writers' groups are made up of a small number of avid writers with vastly different interests, while the writers in organizations all have an interest in the same genre. Both can be very helpful to new writers in terms of support. To find the writers' group in your community, try the library or your city hall.

Visit Your Local Bookstore

One of the *very best* ways of finding market information is to do some of your own research. This might mean nothing more than spending an hour or so in your bookstore, looking through books to find out who publishes the sort of book you've written and copying down any information that might be helpful to you from the books' copyright pages.

Alternatively, you might spend some time leafing through a few magazines, reading bits of the stories therein and deciding if they publish the sort of thing you write. Copy down the name of the magazine's editor and the publication's address (or better still, buy a copy) and send off your story.

Online Resources/Informative Sites

Just as going to the bookstore and checking out the racks for potential markets is a good idea, so too is surfing the Web for horror-fiction markets. There are countless e-zines on the Web, each one open to work by new writers, and their numbers are growing.

DarkEcho Newsletter

DarkEcho is a free weekly electronic newsletter that carries a surprisingly large amount of information about the horror genre. It usually begins with a profile of an author or someone working in the horror field, or an editorial by *DarkEcho* editor Paula Guran. From there it lists horror news from all corners of the globe, including regular updates on horror-movie production in Hollywood, reviews of books and films, and new market listings. In 1999 *DarkEcho* received the Bram Stoker Award from the Horror Writers Association for superior achievement in a work of nonfiction.

For more information, write to <DarkEcho@aol.com>.

Hellnotes

Hellnotes is published 52 times a year by Phantasm Press and features horror news, reviews of horror books and films, and profiles of people working in the horror genre. *Hellnotes* is published by David B. Silva, but reviews and articles are written by several regular contributors. Most interesting about *Hellnotes* is that it is available in a number of different formats (e-mail, fax, snail mail) in escalating subscription prices.

For more information, visit <www.hellnotes.com>, or write to —

Hellnotes
David B. Silva, Editor
27780 Donkey Mine Road
Oak Run, CA
USA 96069

The Chiaroscuro

The Chiaroscuro is more than 700 members strong, is constantly growing, and has been a popular member of the Internet community for more than two years, drawing on 34 countries for its membership. These members include many successful authors, artists, and editors in the dark-fiction genre.

For more information, visit <http://gothic.net/chiaroscuro>.

DarkTales Online Horror Community

On the DarkTales Online Horror Community Web site, everything is horror. DarkTales features Horror Infobase, in which you can search online for your favorite horror information; the Horror Auction, which is an all-horror auction house where you can buy or sell horror books/products/collectibles; and the DarkTales Chatroom, where you can chat with professional horror writers.

For more information, visit <www.darktales.com>.

Other Online Market Listings

The following sites provide some market information on a regular basis, and some, like the Market List and Write Market, are fairly comprehensive sources, which are — best of all — listed free on the Web:

The Market List
<www.marketlist.com>

Speculations
<www.speculations.com>

Write Market
<www.writemarket.com>

Writers Write Paying Market List
<www.writerswrite.com/paying>

Spicy Green Iguana
<members.aol.com/mhatv/index.html>

Trade Magazines

Dark Regions & Horror Magazine

Horror Magazine was started in 1994 as the trade magazine of the horror field. It lasted several issues, then ceased publication, until it was taken over by *Dark Regions* to become *Dark Regions & Horror Magazine,* a quarterly, full-sized magazine featuring horror fiction and poetry; author interviews; reviews of books, films, video, and television; and articles about the horror genre. It's a good mix of fiction and nonfiction, and provides a good overview of the genre.

For more information, write to —

Dark Regions & Horror Magazine
Joe Morey and Ken Wisman, Publishers
Dark Regions Press
PO Box 6301
Concord, CA
USA 94524

Fangoria

Fangoria is the top American magazine devoted to all things horror. Although the magazine has a decided slant toward films and videos, there is some coverage given to authors and there are infrequent reviews of novels and books related to the horror field.

For more information, write to —

Fangoria
475 Park Avenue South
New York, NY
USA 10016

Locus, SF Chronicle

Although *Locus* calls itself "The Newspaper of the Science Fiction Field," this monthly does touch on horror-related subjects and often lists news and market information from the horror field. *SF Chronicle* is also primarily a magazine of the science-fiction field, and publishes on a slightly irregular monthly schedule. Both magazines feature author interviews; news; and news about people in the SF, fantasy, and horror genres; and review dozens of books in each issue.

For more information, visit <www.locusmag.com>, or write to —

Locus
Charles N. Brown, Publisher
PO Box 13305
Oakland, CA
USA 94661
E-mail: <locus@locusmag.com>

SF Chronicle
Andrew I. Porter, Editor and Publisher
PO Box 022730
Brooklyn, NY
USA 11202-0056

Rue Morgue

Rue Morgue is a Canadian publication covering horror film, television, comics, and CDs. It also reviews books and profiles authors and others working in the horror field.

For more information, visit <www.rue-morgue.com>, or write to —

Rue Morgue
1666 St. Clair Avenue West
Toronto, ON
CANADA M6N 1H8

Parsec

Parsec is a Canadian magazine similar to *Rue Morgue* but with an emphasis on Canadian science fiction and fantasy films, television, comics, etc. It does regular reviews of SF books and author profiles, and also publishes fiction.

For more information, visit <www.parsec.on.ca>, or write to —

> *Parsec*
> c/o Plaza 69 Post Office
> 1935 Paris Street
> PO Box 21019
> Sudbury, ON
> CANADA P3E 6G6

14
contracts and agents

So you've just sold a horror story.

Congratulations are in order.

But now that the first wave of joy has crested, it's time to look at the contract and find out what the publisher is asking of you and what he or she is offering in return.

Copyright and Copywrong

Of course, contracts are complicated documents, and it's just not possible to cover everything about them here. In fact, several volumes could be written solely on the subject of short-story contracts. However, there are a few things found within the majority of contracts that every writer should watch out for. Although most contracts are pretty fair in their treatment of writers and usually require nothing more than your signature, there are some clauses of which you should be wary. Luckily, these are not all that difficult to spot if you know what to look for.

The first thing you want to know is how much money (or what, if not money) is being offered for which rights. Money is good, and more money is better, but if you're planning on being in the writing business for a long time (I figure my career's still got a good 40 years to it), getting a little extra money from a publisher now for a bagful of rights that might be worth a great deal years from now might be something to avoid.

In other words... Don't give anything away.

First North American and Other Serial Rights

Most contracts for original stories pay for First North American Serial Rights (FNASR) or First North American Rights (FNAR); in other words, the right to print your story for the first time in North America. In most cases that's all you want to sell to a magazine or anthology. The publishers might reserve the right to reprint the story in a "Best Of" collection or in another of the company's magazines, but they shouldn't be given this right without additional payment. Reserving them this right allows them to plan such a book or alternative publication without you saying no and gumming up their plans. However, if they ever, in fact, want to reprint your story, they would be required to issue you another contract and check in exchange for the reprint rights. (For example, the regular contract for the Canadian magazine *On Spec* reserves reprint rights, but when *On Spec: The First Five Years* was published by Tesseract Books, separate contracts were issued to all the authors involved.)

Some anthology contracts stipulate that in addition to FNAR, the publishers also have nonexclusive world anthology (and audio cassette) rights in all languages. That's all right, too, since the publisher will need that right to sell your story as part of the book to publishers in other countries. If the book sells, you might get a check — providing, of course, that the book has already earned out its initial advance. (That means that the book has already earned back, through sales, the money the publisher paid out before it was published. Publishers don't pay royalties until that money has been recovered. Many times, it never is.) If the book hasn't earned out yet, the money for the foreign sale goes to the publisher and is credited against the advance, helping the book earn out sooner so it can start producing royalties.

The contract will usually also state that the story can't be published elsewhere for six months to a year after its original publication. This ensures that the publisher is buying work that is new and which people won't be able to read elsewhere during the book's early and strongest sales period. Publishers can sometimes be tough on this point, since it is becoming commonplace for big-name writers to sell a story to an anthology and a magazine, which are then published almost simultaneously. Not everyone's work is in such great demand that multiple sales are possible, but if you're a name writer, or if the alternate publication is relatively small, you might be able to make extra sales of the same work.

For example, my short story "Ice Bridge" was simultaneously published in the horror anthology *Northern Frights 4* and the trucking magazine *RPM Canada*. The story appeared in both publications in May 1997. Both editors were aware of the other publication, but were unconcerned about it because neither publication was competing against the other for readers. In fact, *Northern Frights* editor Don Hutchison was actually pleased that I had been able to sell the story again. It is important to note that both editors knew the story would be published elsewhere in the same month. If you try to sell a story twice thinking that no one will know, think again. Doing things like that without an editor's knowledge is a good way to get a bad reputation among the people to whom you're trying to sell your work.

Another way to deal with the exclusivity clause is to simply write the editor a polite letter asking that permission be granted for a story to be reprinted earlier than the date for which the contract allows. It might seem to be a commonsense thing to do, but there have been instances in which stories sold to anthologies that turn out to have lead times of a year or more have been sold and published elsewhere before the anthology has gone to print, leaving editors no choice but to drop the story from the anthology.

When I was preparing my collection, *Death Drives a Semi*, I wanted to include the story "The Rug." The contract for the story was signed April 4, 1995, but the book it was to be published in, *Robert Bloch's Psychos* wasn't published until January 1998. That meant that I wouldn't be able to reprint the story until January 1999, almost four years after signing the contract, which was a problem as my collection was scheduled to be published in October 1998. So I wrote a letter to Martin H. Greenberg, who was putting the *Psychos* book together, and politely asked if I might reprint the story early. Not only did he agree to my request, he congratulated me on the publication of my single-author collection.

Work-for-Hire Contracts

Fortunately, most short-story contracts are pretty reasonable, including work-for-hire contracts issued by companies that own the universe in which your story is set.

Let's say you're commissioned to write a story about Freddy Krueger or Jason. Since the characters you're writing about are owned by their creator or the film company that the produced the films, your story will also become their property. Fortunately, you are usually well paid for such stories, and most work-for-hire contracts recognize that the author has some claim to the story and should be compensated whenever the story is reprinted or used again in some other form.

For example, I've sold several stories to the White Wolf Game Studio, which produces such role-playing games as *Vampire: The Masquerade* and *Mage: The Ascension*. The stories were published in paperback anthologies produced by the Atlanta-based company. However, while the story is theirs to do with as they please, they can't reprint it over and over again without compensating me for each time it sees print. In addition, while I gave up the rights to the characters I created in the stories, the contracts stipulate that if they use my characters in anything else (another person's novel, a gaming module, etc.), I will be paid for that use. The contract also includes a share of royalties on the sale of the anthology and the right to reprint the story in a single-author collection.

This last item is an important one. If you're like most writers, you might dream of having a single-author collection at some point in your career and would hate to lose the right to call a story your own. More important, however, is that if a collection of your own does become a reality, you won't get hung up trying to get permission to reprint your story.

For example, I sold a work-for-hire story to Dark Horse Comics, which was well-paid for but never printed. The contract stated I could reprint the story in a collection three years after its publication in a Dark Horse Comic. Unfortunately, the story was not printed in the first four issues of the comic, and the series was canceled after the fourth issue. What to do? I sent a letter asking for permission to reprint the story (not just in my collection, but in another magazine) and after a while I did indeed get that permission — in writing.

I've yet to reprint the story, but I can if I ever find a market for it.

Contract Watch: What to Look for

What should you look out for in a short-story contract?

Three things.

First, make certain you're not signing a contract that's a blatant rights grab (i.e., an offer of a flat fee for your story in return for granting the publisher *all* rights). If you do this, you are selling your *story* and not the *right to publish your story*. These contracts usually come from companies that are unfamiliar with publishing or are coming into publishing from another business in which rights grabs are common.

(For example, several years ago a military role-playing game company in Pennsylvania put out guidelines asking for alternative-history military SF stories, and offering to buy all rights in return for the equivalent of a cup of coffee and a donut. The warning bells went off everywhere (among writers' organizations and on the Web) and the guidelines were laughed out of cyberspace.)

Second, asking the question, "What if?" will help ensure you're not selling rights that don't yet exist. Say the contract for a classic 1960s horror novel included the purchase of electronic rights (CD ROM, video game, etc.). In the early 1960s they were still coping with electricity, so the author might have been inclined to sell those rights for an added fee (say $100–$5,000) and thought he'd pulled the wool over the publisher's eyes. However, now, 30 years later, those rights might be worth millions.

The other thing about asking "What if?" is that it might prevent you from getting short-changed by a loophole. One short-story contract of mine gave the publisher the right to reprint my story in the anthology "for so long as the Anthology shall remain in print with (the publisher) in any format." What if they film the anthology as a movie, or produce an audio book, or do a mass-market version of the book. What if? Would that mean that they owned the rights to the story in those other (quite lucrative) formats?

Another time "What if?" came in handy was when my first chapbook short-story collection, *Virtual Girls: The Erotic Gems of Evan Hollander*, was published. It included this clause: "To facilitate keeping the Work in print, the Publisher will pay half the regular royalty rate of copies sold from print runs of 100 copies or less." What if the book was successful and they printed 100 copies a week for the next year? After 52 printings, I'd end up with half the royalty on 5,200 copies. I struck out the clause, then signed the contract.

Third, and finally, you should look for a clause that states the following: "The Publisher acknowledges that all rights to the Work not expressly granted by the Author to the Publisher are reserved to the Author." That protects you from losing some rights you didn't realize you were signing away because you didn't ask yourself "What if?" It also protects you from losing rights to things that don't yet exist, like Fliegelman Rights. Who knows? They could be very valuable some day.

These are just a few basic things to watch out for in a short-story contract. Of course, the best thing a writer has going for him or her is commonsense and the ability to read. Read every contract through in its entirety before signing it. If something doesn't feel right, or if you don't understand something, then ask the publisher to explain it to you.

It's vitally important that you know what you're signing. You can always put your signature on the contract, but you can't always take it off.

Where to Get Advice

If you're not sure about something in a contract there are people you can ask for advice.

If you belong to a writers' organization, you can call, e-mail, or write a letter to another member and ask his or her opinion on the matter, which will allow you the benefit of consulting with someone who has far more experience than you do and will provide you with practical advice as it relates to the genre. If you are a member of the Horror

Writers Association, for example, you may be able to get advice from someone who has already dealt with the same magazine or publisher of which you're unsure. Science Fiction and Fantasy Writers of America allows new writers to join as active members (full voting membership) after the writer has been offered a contract and before it has been signed. Therefore, a new member can join and receive the benefits of membership (and the advice of more experienced writers) before he or she has unknowingly signed a bad contract.

If you're not a member of any writers' organization you can still approach a professional writer who you've met at a convention or some other function. Just be sure you're in need of advice on a writing matter and not looking for information that you yourself can easily obtain by spending a few hours in the library. I've been called dozens of times by total strangers who have seen my name or photo in the newspaper who want to know where a friend can send his or her novel, or by someone who has a great idea for a story but needs someone else to write it. There's a world of difference between that sort of question and, "I've just sold a novel to NewAuthor Publishing. Is $250 a decent advance for a first novel?"

When Do You Need an Agent?

New writers also often approach me at writing conferences and ask, "How do I get an agent?"

My response is, "Why do you need an agent?"

Usually, they have just finished writing a book — or worse still, are halfway through a book — and will be needing an agent to sell it for them. More often than not, these writers want to be represented by an agent so their careers as "writers" (unpublished writers at that) will have some sort of validation.

Here are some things to remember about agents:

- If you're selling only short stories, you don't need an agent.

- If you haven't sold anything yet, you probably won't be able to get an agent who's worth having anyway.

- Stay away from agents who go advertising for clients at writers' conventions. Any agent worth having has a full list of clients and is selective about taking on new ones.

A Few Words With...

**Horror Writers Association President
S.P. Somtow**

on the value of the hwa to aspiring horror writers

EDO VAN BELKOM: How could a young horror writer benefit by joining the Horror Writers Association (HWA)? What does HWA have to offer?

S.P. SOMTOW: One can speak of many tangible benefits. The awards, the networking, the address lists, the newsletter, the sharing of marketing information; but the greatest single benefit of membership in the HWA is, I believe, the sense of community and solidarity that membership brings. You know there are people going through the same things you're going through; people you can share with; people who understand the curious nature of your artistic vision. One of the greatest advantages of a field like ours is that the more established writers have always been there to lend a hand up to the next generation. As a writer of SF, fantasy, and horror, it was my privilege to come to know as friends people who were my childhood idols — Isaac Asimov, Ted Sturgeon, and Robert Bloch — and to have these late, great writers actually share with me the benefit of their experience. You are part of a continuum in HWA, and even as a beginner, you will still feel that you belong to the greater cosmos of professionalism.

EDO VAN BELKOM: Many people feel that the horror genre is in a slump, but the membership of HWA seems to be remain at a constant level in terms of numbers. How can you explain that?

S.P. SOMTOW: Writers come and go; there's no question of that. But there is always horror. The Neolithic hunter huddled in his cave knew stories of dark forces. This literature has its origins in mankind's most primal feelings. Whether it is packaged in black covers and put in a specific part of the bookstore or not is about marketing; that is the thing that booms and busts. The literature itself is a constant.

EDO VAN BELKOM: What if a writer is working toward a first sale, but hasn't made one yet. Can he or she still join HWA? Do writers have to write prose fiction, or do other media qualify for membership as well?

S.P. SOMTOW: We have a poetry caucus to recommend whether a poet's work qualifies him or her for active membership. We accept as members screenwriters and nonfiction writers. My policy as president is to make the tent big enough to contain every professional with an abiding interest in this field. Our interpretation of the requirements is strict in the sense that credits must be professional ones rather than self-publishings or giveaways, but within those parameters, the Membership Chair has a lot of leeway to make judgment calls about what does or does not constitute a genre contribution.

In addition to being HWA President, S.P. Somtow is the author of the classic horror novels Vampire Junction, Darker Angels, *and* Moon Dance, *as well as about 40 other books. He is also a composer, a screenwriter, and principal guest conductor of the Bangkok Symphony Orchestra.*

• Do not pay any agent a reading fee. Legitimate agents make their money by selling the work of an author and charging that author a modest 10 percent to 15 percent commission. Reading fees are scams run by fly-by-night agents, who take on clients but never sell anything to publishers. They make their money by charging reading fees to prospective clients, and often recommend "editing" services that will take your money (often thousands of dollars) in return for "editing" your book, which in the end won't make the manuscript any more salable. Keep this in mind: *Money always flows from the publisher to the writer, never the other way around.*

Most book publishers these days will not look at either unsolicited or unagented manuscripts. That narrows the potential markets for your new novel somewhat, but it doesn't eliminate them completely. There's nothing to stop you from writing a polite query letter to an editor, explaining who you are, that you've finished a novel, and could you please send along an outline and a few sample chapters. This gives the editor the chance to refuse you or to agree to look at the outline and sample chapters. If the editor likes what he or she sees, then he or she might ask to see the entire manuscript. Now your manuscript is no longer unsolicited: it has been solicited by the editor. Of course, this is a long, hard way to go about it, but selling a novel is very difficult. I've seen numbers that suggest that only 1 in every 10,000 novels written is ever published, and the true ratio is probably much higher. Writing a novel is difficult, selling it is even harder, but if you give up after the first couple (or 100) rejections, then you might not be cut out to be a writer in the first place.

Getting an Agent

Obviously, at some point in your writing career, you might require the services of an agent. But when?

When I completed my first novel, and after having published something like 30 or more stories, I decided it might be time to acquire an agent. And so, through my membership in the Science Fiction and Fantasy Writers of America, I looked in the directory and found out which agents represented which writers. Then I selected a top agent and wrote a letter asking if he'd like to look at my novel. He answered positively, read the novel and declined to represent it.

It was just as well because the book wasn't good enough for publication. Looking back on it now, I probably would not have been represented as well as I would like to be by an agent with a long client list and a lot of big names on that list.

Agents make money by selling the work of the authors they represent. Obviously, an agent will spend the most time on those authors that make the most money for him or her, and will spend less time on those authors that have less of a chance of doing so. After that first effort, I tried the same agent again with another novel sometime later, and he refused to represent that one as well, saying it would be a difficult book to sell. In other words, the book might sell someday, but it wouldn't be worth the effort to him to sell it. It's a bit of a Catch-22 situation: an agent wants a new author to have a book that's easy to sell before taking him or her on as a client; however, a book that's easy to sell doesn't really need an agent to represent it.

I forgot about getting an agent for a while, and got a commission to write my first published novel, *Wyrm Wolf*, without an agent. Since it was a work-for-hire book, there wasn't any point in hiring an agent to take 10 percent of the advance for negotiating a contract that had little room for negotiation. I did the novel, it did well, and about a year later I had two similar novel contracts in hand.

At that time, I was approached by my current agent after he'd read a story of mine in an anthology that two of his clients had edited for Pocket Books. So after trying unsuccessfully to get an agent to represent me, here was one interested in my work. I answered by saying that if the agent wanted to represent me, he had to represent my novel, the one the first agent said would be a tough sell. He read it, liked it, and agreed to represent it. At that point, I told him about the other two contracts I had, and allowed him to negotiate them on my behalf. Since then, I've sold many books through my agent, including that novel (which was indeed a tough sell, but eventually sold after being rejected more than a dozen times).

All of this is a long-winded way of saying that the time to go looking for an agent is after an editor has made an offer on one of your books. You answer by saying, "I'll have my agent call you," at which point you call the agent of your choice and say, "I've just sold a novel. Would you like to represent me?" Any agent would be a fool to turn down such a proposition.

Marketing Yourself

Many successful professional writers don't use agents at all. A new trend in contract negotiations is to use a lawyer who specializes in publishing and copyright law who will negotiate a book contract for you and charge a fee for his or her services. This might cost more up front, but the lawyer won't be taking 10 percent of your royalties over the book's entire lifetime in print.

Some other writers don't use agents or lawyers at all, but negotiate their own book contracts. (One famous author even provides his own contracts whenever he sells a short story.) This works up to a point, but once the money amounts get large enough, the editor-author relationship can easily become strained over money — as do many relationships.

And here is where the true benefit of having an agent to negotiate contracts and hound publishers for money on your behalf comes into play. The agent can pester and pursue people for money for you, haggle over a few dollars, and get into name calling, but once the contract is signed, you are able to work with the editor without any of the animosity of the negotiating process clouding the working relationship.

15
a final word

So that covers it, just about everything that I could possibly tell you about writing horror fiction. (It's a bit of a revelation, how little you really know about something when you have to sit down and articulately write an entire book on the subject.)

I hope the message that comes through these words is that writing horror or any other kind of fiction is hard work. In reading through all the advice contained in this book, remember that these are very basic tips, things that have worked for me and other writers I know. There are probably all sorts of examples of people who've succeeded in the genre doing things exactly opposite to the ways I've suggested in this book. I wouldn't be surprised; there's always an exception to every rule. Just consider all this a general compilation of the things that have worked most often for the majority of writers.

But of all the bits of wisdom that you might gain from reading this book, the most important one is the simplest.

Writing is hard work.

And it takes three Ds: Drive, Desire, and Determination.

Read a lot.

Write a lot.

Work hard at it.

Stay at it.

Above all, don't let yourself get too discouraged. Just about everyone who has succeeded at the writing game — including the likes of Stephen King and Dean Koontz — have struggled and had moments when it all seemed like madness to continue pursuing a career as a writer. If you can get past those times, believe in yourself, and carry on, then you're halfway toward your goal.

And even if you never publish a thing, just remember that writing and finishing a piece of fiction is an accomplishment in itself.

When you've finished something (a story, novel, or whatever), take the time to congratulate yourself on a job well done, because there will be more than enough people who'll be all too willing to tell you otherwise later on.

All the best.

And best of luck.

appendix 1
WRITERS'
ORGANIZATIONS

Writers' organizations can put you in touch with other writers who are struggling to sell their work, just as you are, or can connect you with established pros who can provide you with advice based on their experiences. Most writers' organizations have quarterly or monthly newsletters and host annual general meetings or meetings of local chapters. While every attempt has been made to ensure the following information is accurate, in writers' organizations, contact information can change often because of the makeup of the people who run them, who are primarily volunteers.

Horror Writers Association

PO Box 50577
Palo Alto, CA
USA 94303
Web site: www.horror.org

Begun in 1984 under the name HOWL (The Horror and Occult Writers League), HWA is the only international organization for people who work within the field of horror. The word "writers" appears in the name of the organization, but membership is open to artists and illustrators, poets, reviewers, book publishers, and agents who work in the horror field. There are several classes of membership, from affiliate to active, but all members receive a newsletter, market updates, and announcements via an Internet mailer. HWA has a presence at most horror conventions and presents the Bram Stoker Awards (voted on by active members of the association) each year.

Science Fiction and Fantasy Writers of America

PO Box 171
Unity, ME
USA 04988-0171
Web site: www.sfwa.org

An association of professional science fiction and fantasy writers, founded in 1965 to inform its membership on matters of professional interest, to promote their general welfare, and to help them deal effectively with publishers, editors, and anthologists. This organization is of interest to horror writers whose work is mainly in the dark-fantasy realm. Publishes a quarterly magazine, *The Bulletin,* the members-only *Forum,* as well as online updates via the Internet. SFWA has a presence at most major SF conventions and hosts annual events such as the Nebula Awards Banquet and the Author/Editors reception in New York City. Presents the Nebula Awards (voted on by the active members of the organization) each year.

SF Canada

Web site: www.sfcanada.ca

An association of Canadian professional science fiction and fantasy writers similar to SFWA, but has less stringent membership requirements.

Mystery Writers of America

17th East 47th Street, 6th Floor
New York, NY
USA 10017
Phone: (212) 888-8171
Fax: (212) 758-8107
E-mail: mwa_org@earthlink.net
Web site: www.mysterywriters.net

One of the oldest and largest mystery-writers' organizations. It has an international membership, with membership categories for published mystery writers, editors, booksellers, and writers in other fields; and pre-published writers who can demonstrate (via copies of query letters, rejection slips, verification of enrollment in courses) that they are serious about their work. Presents the Edgar Allan Poe Awards annually in New York City. MWA maintains a resource library for members, including a listing, available by mail order, of documents on crime-related topics. Mystery and horror often cross the line between the genres, especially when serial killers are involved.

Crime Writers of Canada

3007 Kingston Road
Box 113
Scarborough, ON
CANADA M1M 1P1
E-mail: ap113@freenet.toronto.on.ca

The Crime Writers of Canada is the association for writers of mystery, crime fiction, and crime nonfiction in Canada. You don't have to be Canadian to join, and you don't necessarily have to have sold a work of mystery to be a member. Reviewers and others who work in areas that are related to the mystery and crime fields are welcome. The Crime Writers of Canada puts on events throughout the year such as "Devil of a Good Read" and other readings, and presents the Arthur Ellis Awards at a yearly banquet, usually in Toronto. As an example of the cross between the mystery and horror fields, my short story "The Rug," originally published in the Horror Writers Association anthology *Robert Bloch's Psychos,* was both a Bram Stoker Award nominee and a finalist for the Arthur Ellis Award.

Canadian Authors Association

PO Box 419
Campbellford, ON
CANADA K0L 1L0
Phone: (705) 653-0323
Fax: (705) 653-0593
E-mail: canauth@redden.on.ca
Web site: www.canauthors.org

An organization dedicated to the support and development of Canadian writing in all genres. Its slogan is "Writers helping writers." While the CAA is a national organization and hosts an annual meeting, there are many regional chapters across Canada. The CAA has a category of membership for aspiring writers.

appendix 2
reference books

Writers not only need to read within the field in which they want to work, they must also read about the work itself. Fortunately, there have been a great many books on horror writing and about writing in general published over the years, so finding books on both subjects isn't too difficult a task.

Books about Writing

Applebaum, Judith. *How to Get Happily Published.* 5th edition. New York: HarperCollins, 1998.

Bloch, Robert. *Once around the Bloch: An Unauthorized Autobiography.* New York: Tor Books, 1993.

Block, Lawrence. *Telling Lies for Fun and Profit: A Manual for Fiction Writers.* New York: Arbor House, 1981; Quill, William Morrow, 1994.

Block, Lawrence. *Spider Spin Me a Web: A Handbook for Writers.* New York: William Morrow, 1988.

Card, Orson Scott. *How to Write Science Fiction and Fantasy.* Cincinnati, OH: Writer's Digest Books, 1990.

Castle, Mort, ed. *The Horror Writers Association: Writing Horror.* Cincinnati, OH: Writer's Digest Books, 1996.

Golden, Christopher, ed. *Cut! Horror Writers on Horror Film.* New York: Berkeley Books, 1992.

Kies, Cossette N. *Presenting Young Adult Horror Fiction.* Boston: Twayne Publishing, 1992.

Killian, Crawford, *Writing Science Fiction and Fantasy.* North Vancouver, BC: Self-Counsel Press, 1998.

Lucke, Margaret, *Writing Mysteries.* North Vancouver, BC: Self-Counsel Press, 1999

Stine, R.L. *It Came from Ohio: My Life as a Writer.* New York: Scholastic, 1997.

Sullivan, Jack, ed. *The Penguin Encyclopedia of Horror and the Supernatural.* New York: Viking Penguin, 1986.

Van Belkom, Edo. *Northern Dreamers: Interviews with Famous Writers of Science Fiction, Fantasy and Horror.* Kingston, ON: Quarry Press, 1998.

Wiater, Stan. *Dark Thoughts on Writing.* Grass Valley, CA: Underwood Books, 1997.

Williamson, J.N., ed. *How to Write Horror, Fantasy and Science Fiction.* Cincinnati, OH: Writer's Digest Books, 1987.

Bradbury, Ray. *Zen in the Art of Writing.* Capra Press, 1990; Bantam Books, 1992.

Books about Horror

Copper, Basil. *The Vampire in Legend, Fact and Art.* Corgi Books, 1973.

Daniels, Les. *Living in Fear: A History of Horror in the Mass Media.* New York: Charles Scribners' Sons, 1975.

Douglas, Drake. *Horror!* The MacMillan Company, 1966; New York: Collier Books 1969.

Jones, Stephen, and Kim Newman, eds. *Horror: The 100 Best Books.* New York: Carroll and Graff, 1988 (Updated 1998).

King, Stephen. *Danse Macabre.* New York: Everest House, 1981; New York: Berkeley Books, 1983.

Laymon, Richard. *A Writers Tale.* Apache Junction, AZ: Deadline Press, 1998.

Pringle, David, ed. *Modern Fantasy: The Hundred Best Novels.* Toronto, ON: Grafton Books, 1988.

Underwood, Tim, and Chuck Miller, eds. *Bare Bones: Conversations on Terror with Stephen King.* New York: McGraw Hill, 1988.

Underwood, Tim, and Chuck Miller, eds. *Feast of Fear: Conversations with Stephen King*. New York: Carroll & Graf, 1992.

Wiater, Stan. *Dark Dreamers*. New York: Avon, 1990.

Wiater, Stan. *Dark Visions*. New York: Avon, 1992.

Winter, Douglas E. *Faces of Fear*. New York: Berkeley Books, 1985.

appendix 3
seminal works of horror

If you're like most people, you don't have a lot of time in the day for reading, so you have to choose your reading material carefully. I've mentioned before that many books written about the horror genre contain lists of best or seminal works in the field. If you're interested in taking a look at those lists, here are a few books in which you'll find them.

Castle, Mort, ed. *The Horror Writers Association: Writing Horror*. Cincinnati, OH: Writer's Digest Books, 1996.

(Contains a list of 21 "must read" books for anyone wanting to write within the horror genre.)

Horror Writers Association Handbook and Directory. The Horror Writers Association, Spring 1997.

(Contains of list of "Recommended Reading: The Top 40 Horror Books of All Time.")

Jones, Stephen, and Kim Newman, eds. *Horror: The 100 Best Books*. New York: Carroll and Graff 1988 (Updated 1998).

(In addition to the comprehensive list of 100 best books, this book also includes a list of recommended reading that covers the horror genre from 458 BC to 1996.)

King, Stephen. *Danse Macabre*. New York: Everest House, 1981; New York: Berkeley Books, 1983.

(Lists by author roughly 100 books that King believes to have had some impact on the horror genre. Also includes a similar list of horror films.)

Wiater, Stan. *Dark Thoughts on Writing*. Grass Valley, CA: Underwood Books, 1997.

(Contains a list of 113 best books of modern horror fiction, as well as a list of the 39 best horror anthologies.)

Williamson, J.N., ed. *How to Write Horror, Fantasy and Science Fiction*. Cincinnati, OH: Writer's Digest Books, 1987.

(Contains several lists of favorite horror novels and anthologies, compiled by the editor as well as several of the book's contributors.)

Winter, Douglas E. *Faces of Fear*. New York: Berkeley Books, 1985.

(Lists the "Best of Horror Fiction 1951–1985," as well the best horror films during the same period.)

appendix 4
horror/fantasy
awards

Bram Stoker Award

Web site: www.horror.org

The Bram Stoker Awards are selected each year by the membership of the Horror Writers Association, a professional group of writers, editors, artists, and associated members. The awards are presented at the annual general meeting of the Horror Writers Association, recently held in conjunction with the World Horror Convention. The award itself is a plaster cast of a haunted gothic house with creepy-crawlies and monsters hanging out the windows and onto the walls. The winner's name and title of the work are on a metal plaque, hidden by the hinged front door of the house.

Horror Critics Guild Award

The International Horror Critics Guild Awards are selected each year by the membership of the World Horror Convention, a mixture of writers, editors, and horror fans. The award is a green sculpture — about 10 inches high (from the base) — of a humanoid dog with wings, a gargoyle.

World Fantasy Awards

Writers are nominated each year for World Fantasy Awards by the membership of the World Fantasy Convention, and winners are selected by a panel of judges. The word "Fantasy" in the name of the award is somewhat deceiving, since the awards are presented at the annual convention every Halloween weekend and lean more toward dark fiction than traditional fantasy. The award itself is a pewter caricature bust of H.P. Lovecraft, mounted on a wooden base.

Aurora Awards

Web site: www.sentex.net/~dmullin/aurora

The Aurora Awards are the Canadian speculative fiction awards, and are voted for by open, paid ballot. They are awarded to the best English- and French-language works published by Canadian authors and are presented annually at the national SF convention, which is held in a different Canadian city each year. The award is an aluminum sculpture that spells SF from above and is mounted on a wooden base.

appendix 5
horror authors
you should know

If you're a fan of the horror genre, there's a pretty good chance that you've come to it through horror movies and/or the genre's bestselling authors. But while authors such as Stephen King, Dean Koontz, Clive Barker, Anne Rice, and Peter Straub are writing excellent novels and short stories and deserve all the attention they receive, they actually represent a small fraction of the writers who are creating top-flight fiction in the field of horror. Of course, no one can read everything by every author, but if you want to write horror, it is to your advantage to know the work of others in the field.

Here's a list of some top horror authors and their best or best-known works, as well as a brief description of the kind of horror they most often write.

Charles Beaumont. A contemporary of Richard Matheson, Beaumont wrote many scripts for the original *Twilight Zone* television series. He's best known for his story collections, the most recent of which is *Charles Beaumont: Selected Stories*.

Robert Bloch. Author of *Psycho* and other acclaimed novels, he was also an accomplished short-story writer, with the rare ability to combine humor and horror to great effect.

Ray Bradbury. One of the best short-story writers of his day, perhaps one of the best American short-story writers of the century. His most influential collection is *The October Country.* His novels include *Something Wicked This Way Comes* and *Fahrenheit 451.*

Gary Brandner. Famous as the author of *The Howling,* which was made into a series of horror films. Brandner's *Cameron's Closet* was also made into a feature film.

Poppy Z. Brite. One of the hot young writers to appear on the scene in the early 1990s. Brite's work is as disturbing as it is beautifully written. Novels include *Lost Souls, Drawing Blood,* and *Exquisite Corpse.* Brite has also edited two acclaimed anthologies, *Love in Vein* and *Love in Vein II.*

Ramsey Campbell. British writer widely published in the United Kingdom and the United States. Winner of numerous awards, Campbell is the author of hundreds of short stories as well as such outrageously titled novels as *The Face That Must Die* and *The Doll Who Ate His Mother.*

Matthew J. Costello. Now primarily a suspense author, usually in collaboration with F. Paul Wilson on books like *Mirage,* Costello is also the author of the CD-ROMs *The 7th Guest* and *The 11th Hour.* Solo novels include *Homecoming* and *See How She Runs.* Also the author of two *Child's Play* film novelizations.

Harlan Ellison. Primarily known as a science fiction writer, Harlan Ellison is an equally accomplished horror writer. A recipient of the HWA Lifetime Achievement Award, his stories can be found in dozens of collections, including *Deathbird Stories.*

Dennis Etchison. Although he's written several novels, Etchison's best work is in the short-story medium. Two collections of note are *Red Dreams* and *The Dark Country.*

John Farris. Farris sold his first novel in 1956 at the tender age of 18 and has published some 30 novels since. He's best known as the author of *Fury,* which was made into a feature film, and *When Michael Calls,* which was a television movie.

Ray Garton. A prolific writer from California, Garton broke ground in the field with his vampire novel, *Lost Girls.* Garton has also done several film novelizations and writes for young adults under the name Joseph Locke.

Ed Gorman. Master of several genres, including mystery, western, science fiction, and horror, Gorman is at his best writing suspense novels such as *Black River Falls* and *Daughters of Darkness.* Gorman also writes mainstream thrillers under the name E. J. Gorman and science fiction under the name Daniel Ransom.

Charles L. Grant. Likely the best writer of quiet horror in the genre, Grant has written and edited more than 100 books, mostly in the horror field. His best-known novel was *The Pet*, but lately he's gained fame as the author of first *X-Files* tie-in novels, which were *New York Times* bestsellers.

Jack Ketchum. A very visceral novelist, Ketchum (real-name Dallas Mayr) has written several excellent horror/thriller novels, including *Off Season*, *The Girl Next Door*, and *Stranglehold*. Also an accomplished short-story writer.

Nancy Kilpatrick. Known primarily as an author of vampire novels (*Near Death*, *Child of the Night*, *Reborn*), she has also written many erotic horror novels and edited erotic horror anthologies under the pseudonym Amarantha Knight.

Joe R. Lansdale. One of the founders of the Horror Writers Association, Lansdale began by writing horror but has since moved more into the mainstream. Nevertheless, his current suspense novels can be quite terrifying. Recent novels include *Bad Chili*, *The Two-Bear Mambo*, and *Mucho Mojo*. Lansdale also gained recognition for his early short stories, now collected in books such as *By Bizarre Hands* and *Writer of the Purple Rage*.

Richard Laymon. The author of more than 30 horror novels, Laymon is popular in the United Kingdom and Canada, but has been less so in the United States for want of a US publisher. However, he is now being published in the United States by Leisure, so his popularity is sure to rise. Novels include *Bite*, *The Cellar*, and *Darkness, Tell Us*.

Edward Lee. Although splatterpunk has largely gone out of vogue, Edward Lee (real name Lee Seymour) is doing all he can to keep the tradition alive. Lee's work is violent and gross, and horror fans love it. Novels include *Ghouls*, *The Big Head*, *Succubi*, and *Creekers*.

H.P. Lovecraft. Creator of the Cthulhu Mythos and a frequent contributor to *Weird Tales*. Collections of his stories are many, in a wide variety of editions. An influence on many a young writer, including the young Robert Bloch.

Brian Lumley. Began his career writing Cthulhu-type stories, but has since expanded his writing to include straight horror and dark fantasy. Best known for the *Necroscope* series of novels.

Richard Matheson. The films *What Dreams May Come*, *Somewhere in Time*, *The Omega Man*, *The Incredible Shrinking Man*, and *Hell House* were all based on his novels or short stories. Many of his short stories can be found in the *Shock* series of collections.

Robert McCammon. Sold his very first attempt at a novel, *Baal,* and became a prolific and well-regarded author of horror novels, with such follow-up books as *The Night Boat, They Thirst,* and *Stinger.* His more recent works, such as *Boy's Life,* have garnered him the title "Southern Novelist," and he's pretty much turned his back on the horror genre.

David Morrell. Best known as the creator of the character John Rambo, Morrell is also a respected horror novelist with such titles as *The Totem* and *Testament* to his credit.

Andrew Neiderman. Neiderman's work is not as well known under his own name as it is under the name V. C. Andrews. Neiderman has been writing the Andrews books since Virginia Andrews died some years ago. Under his own name, Neiderman has written more than two dozen novels, including *The Devil's Advocate,* which was made into a feature film starring Al Pacino and Keanu Reaves.

Kim Newman. British author of such novels as *Anno Dracula, The Night Mayor,* and *Jago,* Newman has also written several well-regarded nonfiction books in the horror genre, usually in collaboration with anthologist Stephen Jones.

Thomas Tessier. A much under-rated and perhaps under-appreciated writer of tight, suspenseful stories and novels. Two of his best novels are *The Nightwalker* and *Finishing Touches.*

Chet Williamson. A writer whose work is just as at home in the pages of *Playboy* and *The New Yorker,* Williamson has written several good horror novels and many short stories. Has recently expanded his field of operation to include work-for-hire and film novelizations.

J. N. Williamson. A prolific writer through the 1980s with some 30 novels to his credit. Williamson is also the editor of the acclaimed *Masques* series of anthologies, as well as the editor of a how-to book about writing horror and fantasy from Writer's Digest Books.

F. Paul Wilson. A medical doctor, Wilson wrote the landmark vampire novel *The Keep* as well as a string of other horror and science fiction novels. His best stories are collected in *Soft and Others.*

edo van Belkom

Bram Stoker Award winner Edo van Belkom is the author of more than 150 stories of horror, dark fantasy, and mystery, and has published in such magazines as *Parsec, Storyteller, On Spec,* and *RPM,* as well as the anthologies *Shock Rock 2, Fear Itself, Hot Blood 4* and *6, Dark Destiny, Crossing the Line, Truth Until Paradox, The Conspiracy Files, Brothers of the Night, Robert Bloch's Psychos, Year's Best Horror Stories XX, Best American Erotica 1999,* and *Northern Frights 1, 2, 3,* and *4.*

In addition to winning the 1997 Stoker Award from the Horror Writers Association for "Rat Food" (co-authored with David Nickle), he won the Aurora Award (Canada's top prize for speculative writing) in 1999 for the short story "Hockey's Night in Canada." His first horror novel, *Wyrm Wolf,* was a Locus bestseller and a finalist for the 1995 First Novel Bram Stoker Award. Other novels include *Lord Soth, Mister Magick,* and the erotic horror/mystery novel *Teeth,* which will be published by the American publisher Meisha Merlin in the spring of 2001.

His most recent book is the short-story collection, *Death Drives a Semi,* which features 20 of his best stories and was published by Quarry Press in 1998. Nonfiction books include *Northern Dreamers: Interviews with Famous Authors of Science Fiction, Fantasy and Horror,* and *Writing Erotica,* coming in 2001 from Self-Counsel Press. He is also the editor of the anthology *Northern Horror* and of *Be Afraid!*, an anthology of young-adult horror for Tundra Books, a division of McClelland and Stewart

Born in Toronto in 1962, van Belkom graduated from York University with an honors degree in Creative Writing. He worked as a daily newspaper sports and police reporter for five years before becoming a full-time freelance writer in 1992. Since then, he has done a variety of writing-related work, ranging from trivia questions to book reviews, from opinion pieces on professional wrestling to speeches and special letters for Toronto Mayor Mel Lastman. He has taught short-story writing for the Peel Board of Education, worked as an instructor at Sheridan College, and has lectured on horror and fantasy writing at the University of Toronto and Ryerson Polytechnic University. A frequent guest speaker and panelist at writing conferences and conventions in Canada and the United States, van Belkom was Toastmaster of the 1997 World Horror Convention in Niagara Falls, New York.

He lives in Brampton, Ontario, with his wife, Roberta, and his son, Luke.

His Web pages are located at <www.horrornet.com/belkom.htm> and <www.geocities.com/SoHo/Nook/6877/#>.